# Servlets & JavaServer Pages™ Training Course

MARTY HALL

Prentice Hall PTR
Upper Saddle River, New Jersey 07458

# Contents

| | | |
|---|---|---|
| LECTURE 1 | Getting Started | 1 |
| LECTURE 2 | Handling the Client Request: Form Data | 27 |
| LECTURE 3 | Handling the Client Request: HTTP Request Headers | 51 |
| LECTURE 4 | Generating the HTTP Response | 67 |
| LECTURE 5 | Handling Cookies | 87 |
| LECTURE 6 | Session Tracking | 107 |
| LECTURE 7 | Introducing JavaServer Pages | 123 |
| LECTURE 8 | JSP Scripting Elements | 141 |
| LECTURE 9 | The JSP Page Directive: Structuring Generated Servlets | 165 |
| LECTURE 10 | Including Files and Applets in JSP Documents | 195 |
| LECTURE 11 | Using JavaBeans with JSP | 213 |
| LECTURE 12 | Creating Custom JSP Tag Libraries | 235 |
| LECTURE 13 | Integrating Servlets and JavaServer Pages | 273 |
| LECTURE 14 | Servlet and JSP Summary | 293 |

# Lecture 1

# Getting Started

## Agenda

- What servlets are all about
- Advantages of servlets
- What JSP is all about
- Free servlet and JSP engines
- Compiling and invoking servlets
- Servlet structure
- A few basic servlets
- Servlet lifecycle
- Initializing servlets
- Debugging servlets

## Notes:

# LECTURE 1 GETTING STARTED

## A Servlet's Job

- **Read any data sent by the user**
  — From HTML form, applet, or custom HTTP client.
- **Look up HTTP request information**
  — Browser capabilities, cookies, requesting host, etc.
- **Generate the results**
  — JDBC, RMI, direct computation, legacy app, etc.
- **Format the results inside a document**
  — HTML, Excel, etc.
- **Set HTTP response parameters**
  — MIME type, cookies, compression, etc.
- **Send the document to the client**

## Notes:

## Why Build Web Pages Dynamically?

- **The Web page is based on data submitted by the user**
  - E.g., results page from search engines and order-confirmation pages at online stores.
- **The Web page is derived from data that changes frequently**
  - E.g., a weather report or news headlines page.
- **The Web page uses information from databases or other server-side sources**
  - E.g., an e-commerce site could use a servlet to build a Web page that lists the current price and availability of each item that is for sale.

**Notes:**

## The Advantages of Servlets Over "Traditional" CGI

- **Efficient**
  — Threads instead of OS processes, one servlet copy, persistence.
- **Convenient**
  — Lots of high-level utilities.
- **Powerful**
  — Sharing data, pooling, persistence.
- **Portable**
  — Run on virtually all operating systems and servers.
- **Secure**
  — No shell escapes, no buffer overflows.
- **Inexpensive**

## Notes:

## Extending the Power of Servlets: JavaServer Pages (JSP)

- **Idea:**
  — Use regular HTML for most of page.
  — Mark dynamic content with special tags.
  — Details in second half of course.

```
<!DOCTYPE HTML PUBLIC "-//W3C//DTD HTML 4.0 Transitional//EN">
<HTML>
<HEAD><TITLE>Welcome to Our Store</TITLE></HEAD>
<BODY>
<H1>Welcome to Our Store</H1>
<SMALL>Welcome,
<!-- User name is "New User" for first-time visitors -->
<%= Utils.getUserNameFromCookie(request) %>
To access your account settings, click
<A HREF="Account-Settings.html">here.</A></SMALL>
<P>
Regular HTML for  rest of on-line store's Web page
</BODY></HTML>
```

## Notes:

LECTURE 1  GETTING STARTED

## Server-Side Java is Driving the Web

- **Get on board or get out of the way**

**Notes:**

## Free Servlet and JSP Engines

- **Apache Tomcat**
  - http://jakarta.apache.org/tomcat/.
  - See http://archive.coreservlets.com/Using-Tomcat.html.
- **Sun JSWDK**
  - http://java.sun.com/products/servlet/download.html.
- **Allaire JRun**
  - http://www.allaire.com/products/jrun/.
- **New Atlanta ServletExec**
  - http://www.servletexec.com/.
- **Gefion Software LiteWebServer**
  - http://www.gefionsoftware.com/LiteWebServer/.
- **Resin**
  - http://www.caucho.com/.

## Notes:

## Compiling and Invoking Servlets

- **Set your CLASSPATH**
  — Servlet JAR file (e.g., servlet.jar).
  — JSP JAR file (e.g., jasper.jar, jspengine.jar, jsp.jar).
  — Top of your package hierarchy.
- **Put your servlet classes in proper location**
  — Locations vary from server to server. E.g.,
    - *install_dir*/webapps/ROOT/WEB-INF/classes (Tomcat). See http://archive.coreservlets.com/Using-Tomcat.html.
    - *install_dir*/webpages/WEB-INF/servlets (JSWDK).
- **Invoke your servlets**
  — http://host/servlet/ServletName.
  — Server-specific URL-to-servlet mapping.

## Notes:

## Simple Servlet Template

```
import java.io.*;
import javax.servlet.*;
import javax.servlet.http.*;

public class ServletTemplate extends HttpServlet {
  public void doGet(HttpServletRequest request,
                    HttpServletResponse response)
      throws ServletException, IOException {

    // Use "request" to read incoming HTTP headers
    // (e.g. cookies) and HTML form data (query data)

    // Use "response" to specify the HTTP response status
    // code and headers (e.g. the content type, cookies).

    PrintWriter out = response.getWriter();
    // Use "out" to send content to browser
  }
}
```

## Notes:

# LECTURE 1    GETTING STARTED

## A Simple Servlet Generating Plain Text

```
import java.io.*;
import javax.servlet.*;
import javax.servlet.http.*;

public class HelloWorld extends HttpServlet {
  public void doGet(HttpServletRequest request,
                    HttpServletResponse response)
      throws ServletException, IOException {
    PrintWriter out = response.getWriter();
    out.println("Hello World");
  }
}
```

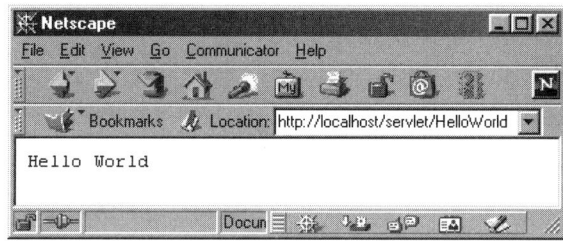

## Notes:

## Compiling and Invoking Servlet (Tomcat 3)

- **Place code in C:\Servlets+JSP**
  — R-click on source code at http://archive.coreservlets.com.
- **CLASSPATH already set**
- **Start DOS; type "javac HelloWorld.java"**
- **Place HelloWorld.class in servlet directory**
  — C:\jakarta-tomcat\webapps\ROOT\WEB-INF\classes.
  — Drag files onto shortcut in Servlets+JSP directory.
- **Start server**
  — Double click startup.bat (C:\jakarta-tomcat\bin).
- **Invoke servlet**
  — http://localhost/servlet/HelloWorld.

## Notes:

## Generating HTML

- **Set the Content-Type header**
  — Use response.setContentType.
- **Output HTML**
  — Be sure to include the DOCTYPE.
- **Use an HTML validation service**
  — http://validator.w3.org/.
  — http://www.htmlhelp.com/tools/validator/.

## Notes:

## A Servlet That Generates HTML

```
public class HelloWWW extends HttpServlet {
  public void doGet(HttpServletRequest request,
                    HttpServletResponse response)
      throws ServletException, IOException {
    response.setContentType("text/html");
    PrintWriter out = response.getWriter();
    String docType =
      "<!DOCTYPE HTML PUBLIC \"-//W3C//DTD HTML 4.0 " +
      "Transitional//EN\">\n";
    out.println(docType +
                "<HTML>\n" +
                "<HEAD><TITLE>Hello WWW</TITLE></HEAD>\n" +
                "<BODY>\n" +
                "<H1>Hello WWW</H1>\n" +
                "</BODY></HTML>");
  }
}
```

## Notes:

## Packaging Servlets

- **Move the files to a subdirectory that matches the intended package name**
  - For example, I'll use the coreservlets package for most of the rest of the servlets in this course. So, the class files need to go in a subdirectory called coreservlets.
- **Insert a package statement in the class file**
  - E.g., top of HelloWWW2.java:
    package coreservlets;
- **Set CLASSPATH to top-level directory**
  - E.g., C:\Servlets+JSP.
- **Include package name in URL**
  - http://localhost/servlet/**coreservlets.**HelloWWW2.

## Notes:

## Some Simple HTML-Building Utilities

```
public class ServletUtilities {
  public static final String DOCTYPE =
    "<!DOCTYPE HTML PUBLIC \"-//W3C//DTD HTML 4.0 " +
    "Transitional//EN\">";

  public static String headWithTitle(String title) {
    return(DOCTYPE + "\n" +
           "<HTML>\n" +
           "<HEAD><TITLE>" + title + "</TITLE></HEAD>\n");
  }
  ...
}
```

- **Don't go overboard**
    — Complete HTML generation packages usually work poorly.
    — The JSP framework is a better solution.

**Notes:**

## HelloWWW with ServletUtilities

```
package coreservlets;

import java.io.*;
import javax.servlet.*;
import javax.servlet.http.*;

public class HelloWWW3 extends HttpServlet {
  public void doGet(HttpServletRequest request,
                    HttpServletResponse response)
      throws ServletException, IOException {
    response.setContentType("text/html");
    PrintWriter out = response.getWriter();
    out.println(ServletUtilities.headWithTitle("Hello WWW") +
                "<BODY>\n" +
                "<H1>Hello WWW</H1>\n" +
                "</BODY></HTML>");
  }
}
```

## Notes:

## HelloWWW Result

## Notes:

## The Servlet Life Cycle

- **init**
  — Executed once when the servlet is first loaded.
    *Not* called for each request.
- **service**
  — Called in a new thread by server for each request. Dispatches to doGet, doPost, etc.
    Do not override this method!
- **doGet, doPost, doXxx**
  — Handles GET, POST, etc., requests.
  — Override these to provide desired behavior.
- **destroy**
  — Called when server deletes servlet instance.
    *Not* called after each request.

## Notes:

## Why You Should *Not* Override Service

- **You can add support for other services later by adding doPut, doTrace, etc.**
- **You can add support for modification dates by adding a getLastModified method**
- **The service method gives you automatic support for:**
  - HEAD requests.
  - OPTIONS requests.
  - TRACE requests.
- **Alternative: have doPost call doGet**

**Notes:**

## Initializing Servlets

- **Common in real-life servlets**
  - E.g., initializing database connection pools.
- **There are two versions of init**
  - One that takes no args; one that takes a ServletConfig.
- **Use ServletConfig.getInitParameter to read initialization parameters**
- **You *read* init params in a portable manner; you *set* them in a server-specific manner**
  - Thus, keep number of params small.
- **It is common to use init even when you don't read init parameters**
  - See modification date example in *Core Servlets and JavaServer Pages* Chapter 2.

## Notes:

## A Servlet Using Initialization Parameters

```java
public class ShowMessage extends HttpServlet {
  private String message;
  private String defaultMessage = "No message.";
  private int repeats = 1;

  public void init(ServletConfig config)
      throws ServletException {
    super.init(config); // Always call super.init
    message = config.getInitParameter("message");
    if (message == null) {
      message = defaultMessage;
    }
    try {
      String repeatString =
        config.getInitParameter("repeats");
      repeats = Integer.parseInt(repeatString);
    } catch(NumberFormatException nfe) {}
  }

  public void doGet(HttpServletRequest request,
                    HttpServletResponse response)
      throws ServletException, IOException {
    response.setContentType("text/html");
    PrintWriter out = response.getWriter();
    String title = "The ShowMessage Servlet";
    out.println(ServletUtilities.headWithTitle(title) +
                "<BODY BGCOLOR=\"#FDF5E6\">\n" +
                "<H1 ALIGN=CENTER>" + title + "</H1>");
    for(int i=0; i<repeats; i++) {
      out.println(message + "<BR>");
    }
    out.println("</BODY></HTML>");
  }
}
```

# Setting Init Parameters in Tomcat 3

- *install_dir*\webapps\ROOT\WEB-INF\web.xml

```xml
<web-app>
  <servlet>
    <servlet-name>ShowMsg</servlet-name>
    <servlet-class>coreservlets.ShowMessage</servlet-class>

    <init-param>
      <param-name>message</param-name>
      <param-value>Shibboleth</param-value>
    </init-param>

    <init-param>
      <param-name>repeats</param-name>
      <param-value>5</param-value>
    </init-param>
  </servlet>
</web-app>
```

## Notes:

## ShowMessage Result

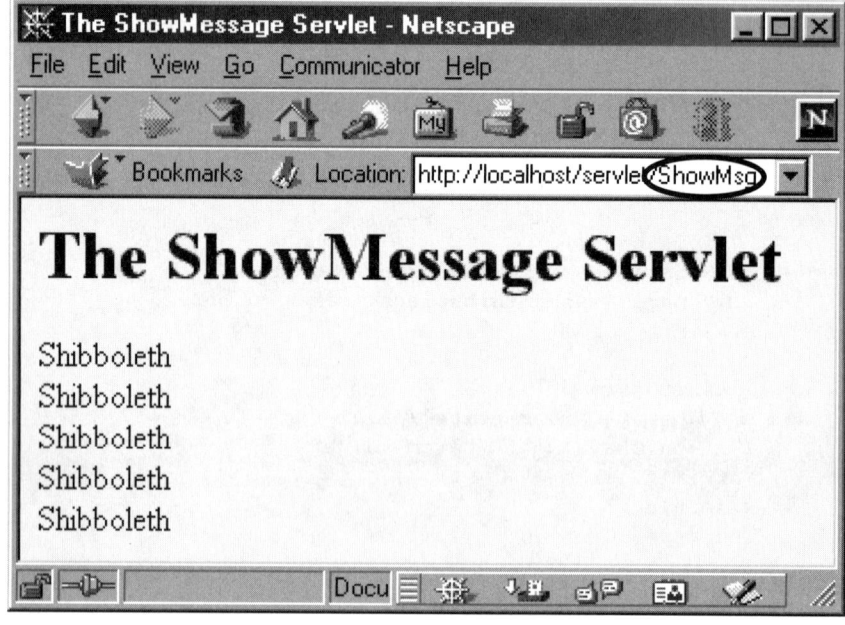

**Notes:**

## Debugging Servlets

- **Use print statements; run server on desktop**
- **Look at the HTML source**
- **Return error pages to the client**
  — See response.sendError later in presentation.
- **Use the log file**
  — log("message") or log("message", Throwable).
- **Look at the request data separately**
  — See EchoServer at www.coreservlets.com.
- **Look at the response data separately**
  — See WebClient at www.coreservlets.com.
- **Stop and restart the server**
- **Integrated debugger in IDE**

**Notes:**

## Summary

- **Servlets are efficient, portable, powerful, and widely accepted in industry**
- **Regardless of deployment server, run a free server on your desktop for development**
- **Getting started:**
  — Set your CLASSPATH.
    - Servlet and JSP JAR files.
    - Top of your package hierarchy.
  — Put class files in proper location.
  — Use proper URL, usually http://*host*/servlet/ServletName.
- **Download existing servlet first time**
  — Start with HelloWWW from www.coreservlets.com.
- **Main servlet code goes in doGet or doPost:**
  — The HttpServletRequest contains the incoming information.
  — The HttpServletResponse lets you set outgoing information.
    - Call setContentType to specify MIME type.
    - Call getWriter to obtain a Writer pointing to client.
- **One-time setup code goes in init**
  — Servlet gets initialized and loaded once.
  — Servlet gets invoked multiple times.

## Notes:

# Lecture 2

# Handling the Client Request: Form Data

## Agenda

- Why form data is important
- Processing form data in traditional CGI
- Processing form data in servlets
- Reading individual request parameters
- Reading all request parameters
- Real-life servlets: handling malformed data
- Filtering HTML-specific characters

## Notes:

## The Role of Form Data

- **Example URL at online travel agent**
  — http://host/path?**user=Marty+Hall&origin=bwi&dest=lax.**
  — Names come from HTML author; values usually come from end user.
- **Parsing form (query) data in traditional CGI**
  — Read the data one way (QUERY_STRING) for GET requests, another way (standard input) for POST requests.
  — Chop pairs at ampersands, then separate parameter names (left of the equal signs) from parameter values (right of the equal signs).
  — URL decode values (e.g., "%7E" becomes "~").
  — Need special cases for omitted values (param1=val1&param2=&param3=val3) and repeated parameters (param1=val1&**param2=**val2&param1=val3).

## Notes:

## Creating Form Data: HTML Forms

```
<!DOCTYPE HTML PUBLIC "-//W3C//DTD HTML 4.0 Transitional//EN">
<HTML>
<HEAD><TITLE>A Sample Form Using GET</TITLE></HEAD>
<BODY BGCOLOR="#FDF5E6">
<H2 ALIGN="CENTER">A Sample Form Using GET</H2>

<FORM ACTION="http://localhost:8088/SomeProgram">
  <CENTER>
  First name:
  <INPUT TYPE="TEXT" NAME="firstName" VALUE="Joe"><BR>
  Last name:
  <INPUT TYPE="TEXT" NAME="lastName" VALUE="Hacker"><P>
  <INPUT TYPE="SUBMIT"> <!-- Press this to submit form -->
  </CENTER>
</FORM>
</BODY></HTML>
```

- See *Core Servlets and JavaServer Pages* Chapter 16 for details on forms

## Notes:

## LECTURE 2 HANDLING THE CLIENT REQUEST: FORM DATA

# HTML Form: Initial Result

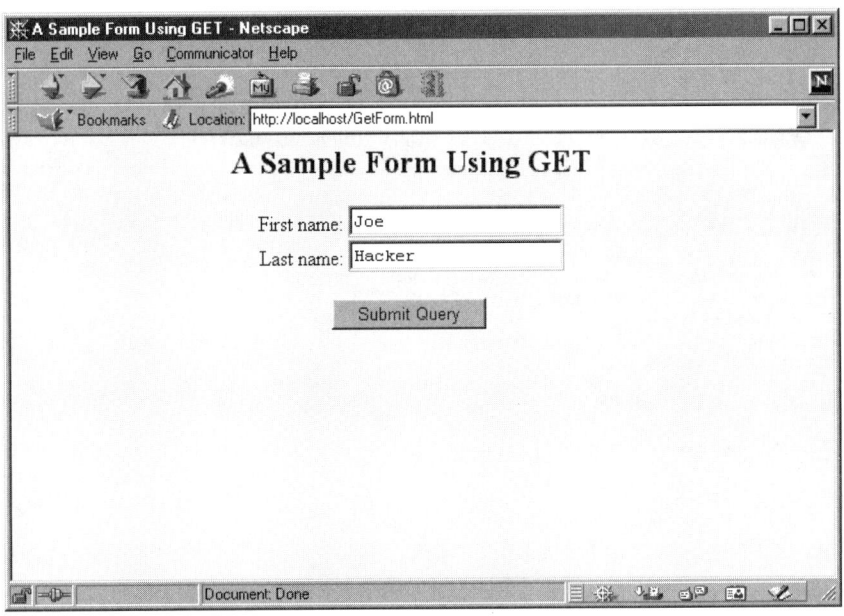

# Notes:

## HTML Form: Submission Result (Data Sent to EchoServer)

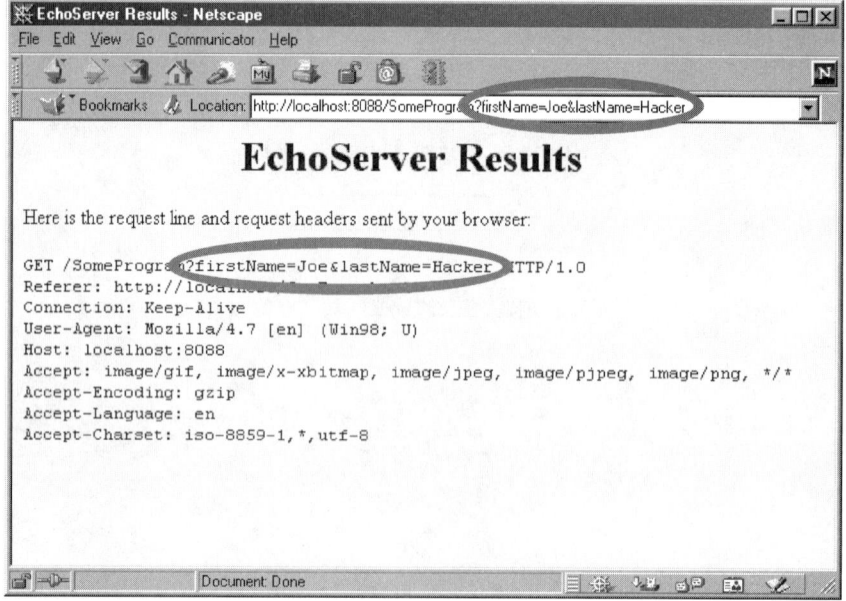

**Notes:**

# LECTURE 2 HANDLING THE CLIENT REQUEST: FORM DATA

## Sending POST Data

```
<!DOCTYPE HTML PUBLIC "-//W3C//DTD HTML 4.0 Transitional//EN">
<HTML>
<HEAD><TITLE>A Sample Form Using POST</TITLE></HEAD>
<BODY BGCOLOR="#FDF5E6">
<H2 ALIGN="CENTER">A Sample Form Using POST</H2>

<FORM ACTION="http://localhost:8088/SomeProgram"
      METHOD="POST">
  <CENTER>
  First name:
  <INPUT TYPE="TEXT" NAME="firstName" VALUE="Joe"><BR>
  Last name:
  <INPUT TYPE="TEXT" NAME="lastName" VALUE="Hacker"><P>
  <INPUT TYPE="SUBMIT">
  </CENTER>
</FORM>

</BODY></HTML>
```

## Notes:

## Sending POST Data

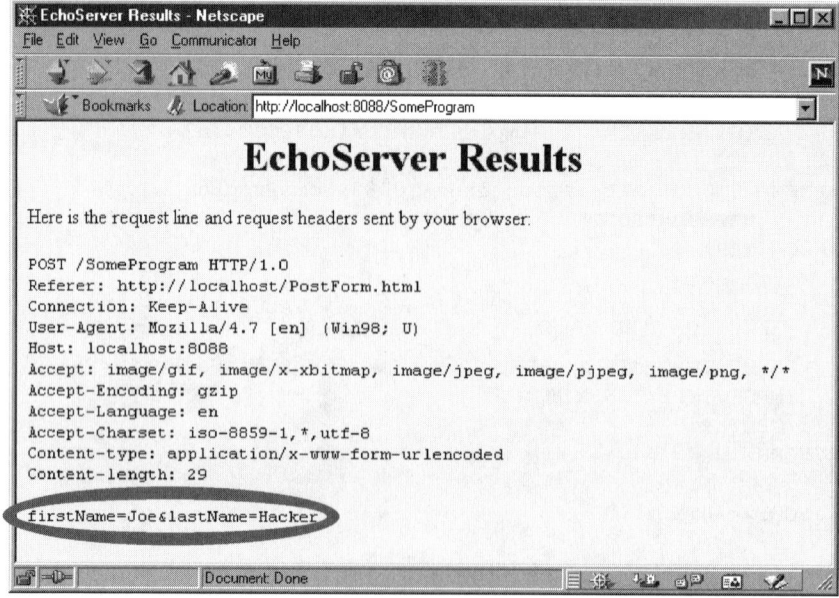

## Notes:

## Reading Form Data in Servlets

- **getParameter("name")**
  - Returns URL-decoded value of first occurrence of name in query string.
  - Works identically for GET and POST requests.
  - Returns null if no such parameter is in query.
- **getParameterValues("name")**
  - Returns an array of the URL-decoded values of all occurrences of name in query string.
  - Returns a one-element array if param not repeated.
  - Returns null if no such parameter is in query.
- **getParameterNames()**
  - Returns Enumeration of request params.

## Notes:

## An HTML Form with Three Parameters

```
<FORM ACTION="/servlet/coreservlets.ThreeParams">
  First Parameter:  <INPUT TYPE="TEXT" NAME="param1"><BR>
  Second Parameter: <INPUT TYPE="TEXT" NAME="param2"><BR>
  Third Parameter:  <INPUT TYPE="TEXT" NAME="param3"><BR>
  <CENTER><INPUT TYPE="SUBMIT"></CENTER>
</FORM>
```

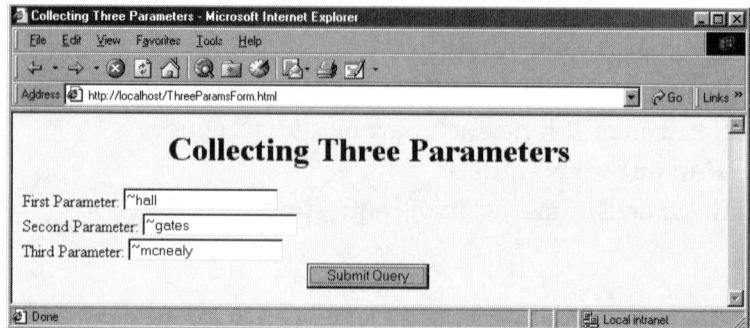

## Notes:

## Reading the Three Parameters

```java
public class ThreeParams extends HttpServlet {
  public void doGet(HttpServletRequest request,
                    HttpServletResponse response)
      throws ServletException, IOException {
    response.setContentType("text/html");
    PrintWriter out = response.getWriter();
    String title = "Reading Three Request Parameters";
    out.println(ServletUtilities.headWithTitle(title) +
                "<BODY BGCOLOR=\"#FDF5E6\">\n" +
                "<H1 ALIGN=CENTER>" + title + "</H1>\n" +
                "<UL>\n" +
                "  <LI><B>param1</B>: "
                + request.getParameter("param1") + "\n" +
                "  <LI><B>param2</B>: "
                + request.getParameter("param2") + "\n" +
                "  <LI><B>param3</B>: "
                + request.getParameter("param3") + "\n" +
                "</UL>\n" +
                "</BODY></HTML>"); }}
```

## Notes:

## Reading Three Parameters: Result

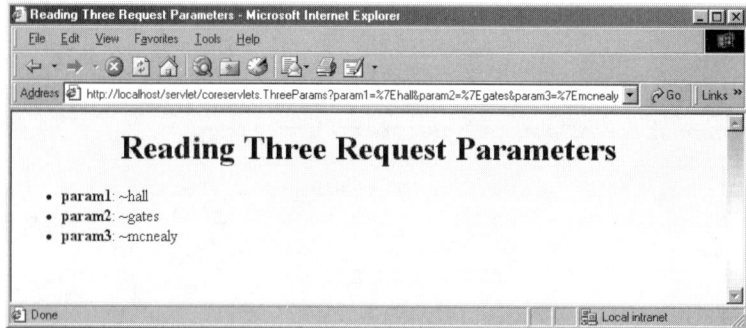

## Notes:

# LECTURE 2  HANDLING THE CLIENT REQUEST: FORM DATA

## Reading All Parameters

```
public class ShowParameters extends HttpServlet {
  public void doGet(HttpServletRequest request,
                    HttpServletResponse response)
      throws ServletException, IOException {
    response.setContentType("text/html");
    PrintWriter out = response.getWriter();
    String title = "Reading All Request Parameters";
    out.println(ServletUtilities.headWithTitle(title) +
                "<BODY BGCOLOR=\"#FDF5E6\">\n" +
                "<H1 ALIGN=CENTER>" + title + "</H1>\n" +
                "<TABLE BORDER=1 ALIGN=CENTER>\n" +
                "<TR BGCOLOR=\"#FFAD00\">\n" +
                "<TH>Parameter Name<TH>Parameter Value(s)");

    Enumeration paramNames = request.getParameterNames();
    while(paramNames.hasMoreElements()) {
      String paramName = (String)paramNames.nextElement();
      out.print("<TR><TD>" + paramName + "\n<TD>");
      String[] paramValues =
        request.getParameterValues(paramName);
      if (paramValues.length == 1) {
        String paramValue = paramValues[0];
        if (paramValue.length() == 0)
          out.println("<I>No Value</I>");
        else
          out.println(paramValue);
      } else {
        out.println("<UL>");
        for(int i=0; i<paramValues.length; i++) {
          out.println("<LI>" + paramValues[i]);
        }
        out.println("</UL>");
      }
    }
    out.println("</TABLE>\n</BODY></HTML>");
  }

  public void doPost(HttpServletRequest request,
                     HttpServletResponse response)
      throws ServletException, IOException {
    doGet(request, response);
  }
}
```

## Result of ShowParameters Servlet

— Note that order of parameters in Enumeration does not match order they appeared in Web page.

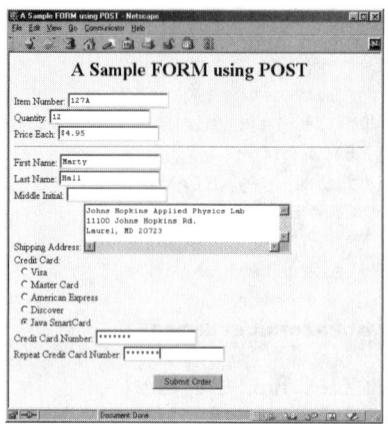 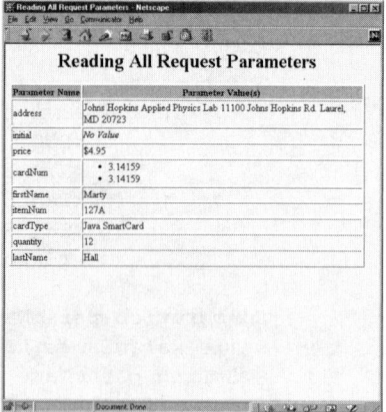

## Notes:

# LECTURE 2 HANDLING THE CLIENT REQUEST: FORM DATA

## Posting Service: Front End

- **Gathers resumé formatting and content information**

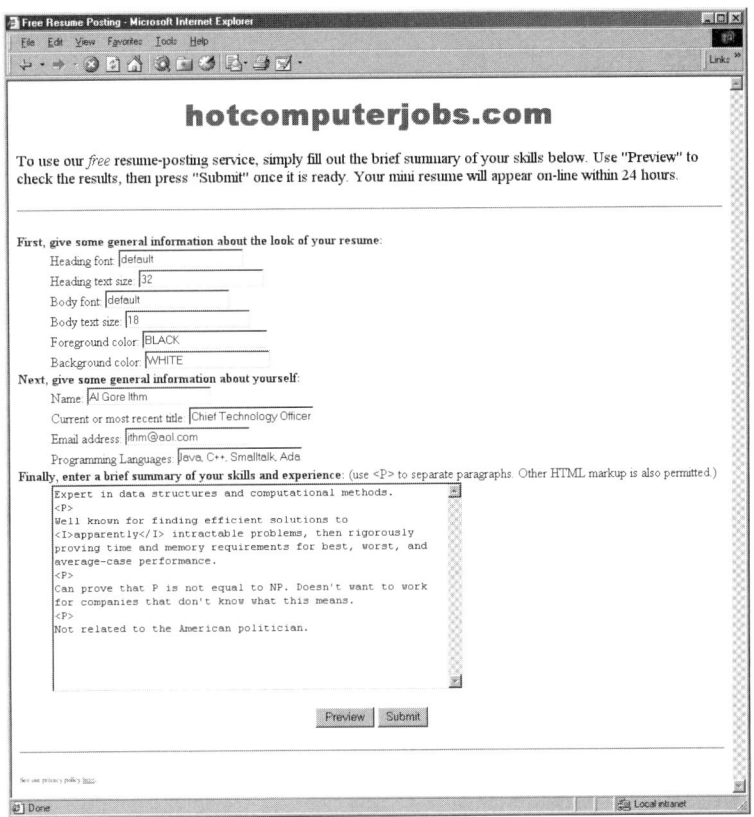

# Posting Service: Back End

- **Previews result or stores resumé in database**

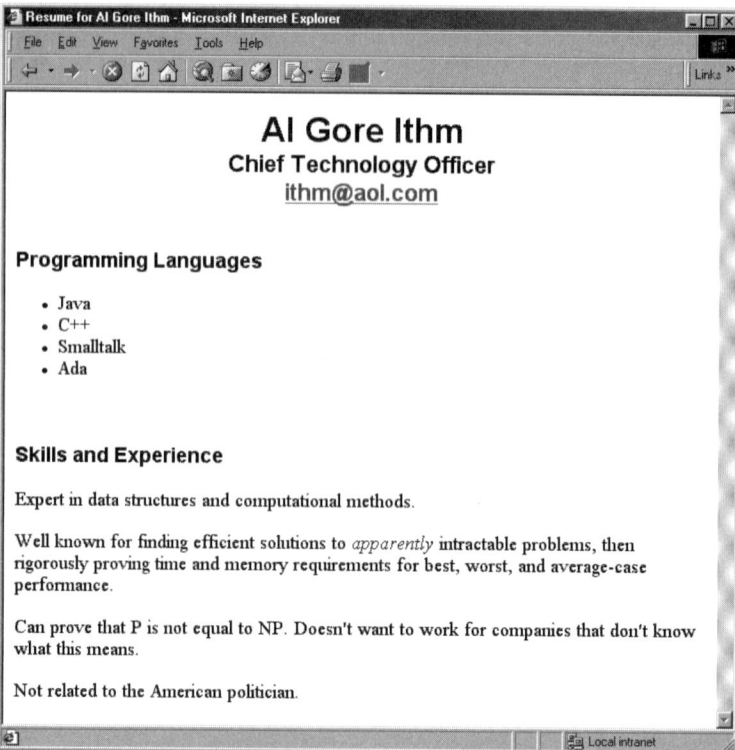

## LECTURE 2 HANDLING THE CLIENT REQUEST: FORM DATA

## Posting Service: Servlet Code

```
private void showPreview(HttpServletRequest request,
                        PrintWriter out) {
  String headingFont = request.getParameter("headingFont");
  headingFont = replaceIfMissingOrDefault(headingFont, "");
  ...
  String name = request.getParameter("name");
  name = replaceIfMissing(name, "Lou Zer");
  String title = request.getParameter("title");
  title = replaceIfMissing(title, "Loser");
  String languages = request.getParameter("languages");
  languages = replaceIfMissing(languages, "<I>None</I>");
  String languageList = makeList(languages);
  String skills = request.getParameter("skills");
  skills = replaceIfMissing(skills, "Not many, obviously.");
  ...
}
```

- **Point: always explicitly handle missing or malformed query data**

## Notes:

## Filtering Strings for HTML-Specific Characters

- **You cannot safely insert arbitrary strings into servlet output**
  - < and > can cause problems anywhere.
  - & and " can cause problems inside of HTML attributes.
- **You sometimes cannot manually translate**
  - The string is derived from a program excerpt or another source where it is already in some standard format.
  - **The string is derived from HTML form data.**
- **Failing to filter special characters from form data makes you vulnerable to *cross-site scripting attack***
  - http://www.cert.org/advisories/CA-2000-02.html.
  - http://www.microsoft.com/technet/security/crssite.asp.

**Notes:**

## Filtering Code (ServletUtilities.java)

```java
public static String filter(String input) {
  StringBuffer filtered = new StringBuffer(input.length());
  char c;
  for(int i=0; i<input.length(); i++) {
    c = input.charAt(i);
    if (c == '<') {
      filtered.append("&lt;");
    } else if (c == '>') {
      filtered.append("&gt;");
    } else if (c == '"') {
      filtered.append("&quot;");
    } else if (c == '&') {
      filtered.append("&amp;");
    } else {
      filtered.append(c);
    }
  }
  return(filtered.toString());
}
```

## Notes:

## Servlet That Fails to Filter

```
public class BadCodeServlet extends HttpServlet {
  private String codeFragment =
    "if (a<b) {\n" +
    "  doThis();\n" +
    "} else {\n" +
    "  doThat();\n" +
    "}\n";

  public String getCodeFragment() {
    return(codeFragment);
  }

  public void doGet(HttpServletRequest request,
                    HttpServletResponse response)
      throws ServletException, IOException {
    response.setContentType("text/html");
    PrintWriter out = response.getWriter();
    String title = "The Java 'if' Statement";

    out.println(ServletUtilities.headWithTitle(title) +
                "<BODY>\n" +
                "<H1>" + title + "</H1>\n" +
                "<PRE>\n" +
                getCodeFragment() +
                "</PRE>\n" +
                "Note that you <I>must</I> use curly braces\n" +
                "when the 'if' or 'else' clauses contain\n" +
                "more than one expression.\n" +
                "</BODY></HTML>");
  }
}
```

## Notes:

_____

_____

_____

_____

## Servlet That Fails to Filter (Result)

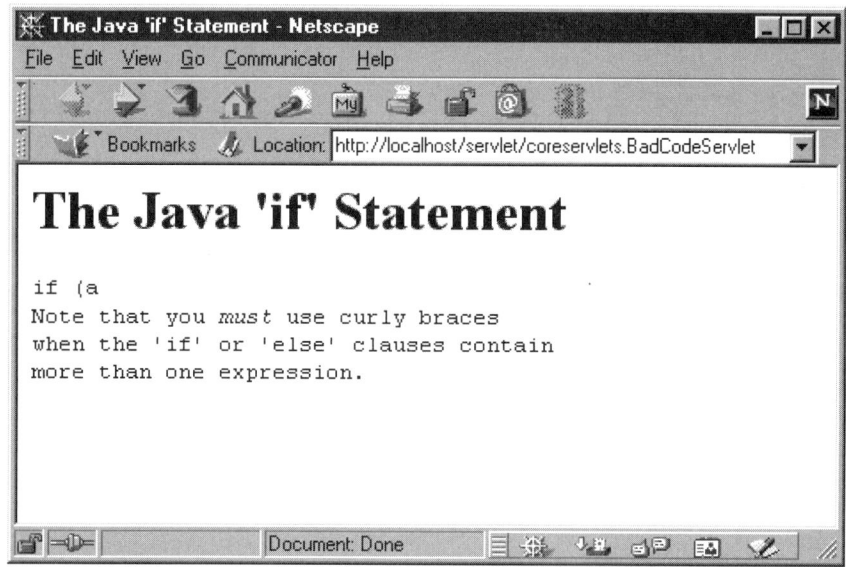

## Notes:

## Servlet That Properly Filters

```
public class FilteredCodeServlet extends BadCodeServlet {
  public String getCodeFragment() {
    return(ServletUtilities.filter(super.getCodeFragment()));
  }
}
```

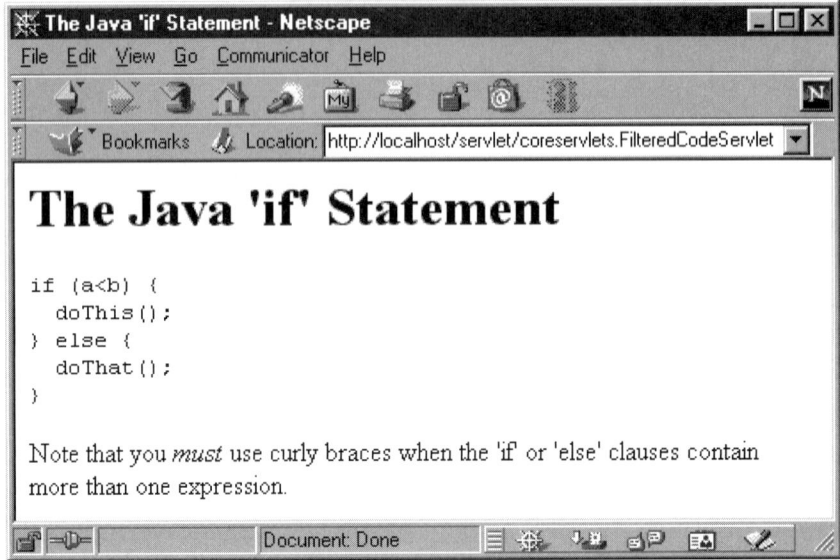

## Notes:

## LECTURE 2  HANDLING THE CLIENT REQUEST: FORM DATA

## Summary

- **Query data comes from HTML forms as URL-encoded name/value pairs**
- **Servlets read data by calling request.getParameter("name")**
  - Results in value as entered into form, not as sent over network. I.e., *not* URL-encoded.
- **Always check for missing or malformed data**
  - Special case: query data that contains special HTML characters.
    - Need to be filtered if query data will be placed into resultant HTML page.

## Notes:

# Lecture 3

# Handling the Client Request: HTTP Request Headers

## Agenda

- Idea of HTTP request headers
- Reading request headers from servlets
- Example: printing all headers
- Common HTTP 1.1 request headers
- Example: compressing Web pages

## Notes:

# LECTURE 3 HANDLING THE CLIENT REQUEST: HTTP REQUEST HEADERS

## Handling the Client Request: HTTP Request Headers

- **Example HTTP 1.1 Request**
  ```
  GET /search?keywords=servlets+jsp HTTP/1.1
  Accept: image/gif, image/jpg, */*
  Accept-Encoding: gzip
  Connection: Keep-Alive
  Cookie: userID=id456578
  Host: www.somebookstore.com
  Referer: http://www.somebookstore.com/findbooks.html
  User-Agent: Mozilla/4.7 [en] (Win98; U)
  ```
- **It shouldn't take a rocket scientist to realize that you need to understand HTTP to be effective with servlets or JSP**

**Notes:**

## Reading Request Headers

- **General**
  - getHeader.
  - getHeaders (2.2 only).
  - getHeaderNames.
- **Specialized**
  - getCookies.
  - getAuthType and getRemoteUser.
  - getContentLength.
  - getContentType.
  - getDateHeader.
  - getIntHeader.
- **Related info**
  - getMethod, getRequestURI, getProtocol.

## Notes:

## LECTURE 3 HANDLING THE CLIENT REQUEST: HTTP REQUEST HEADERS

## Printing All Headers

```java
public class ShowRequestHeaders extends HttpServlet {
  public void doGet(HttpServletRequest request,
                    HttpServletResponse response)
      throws ServletException, IOException {
    response.setContentType("text/html");
    PrintWriter out = response.getWriter();
    String title = "Servlet Example: Showing Request Headers";
    out.println(ServletUtilities.headWithTitle(title) +
                "<BODY BGCOLOR=\"#FDF5E6\">\n" +
                "<H1 ALIGN=CENTER>" + title + "</H1>\n" +
                "<B>Request Method: </B>" +
                request.getMethod() + "<BR>\n" +
                "<B>Request URI: </B>" +
                request.getRequestURI() + "<BR>\n" +
                "<B>Request Protocol: </B>" +
                request.getProtocol() + "<BR><BR>\n" +
                "<TABLE BORDER=1 ALIGN=CENTER>\n" +
                "<TR BGCOLOR=\"#FFAD00\">\n" +
                "<TH>Header Name<TH>Header Value");
    Enumeration headerNames = request.getHeaderNames();
    while(headerNames.hasMoreElements()) {
      String headerName = (String)headerNames.nextElement();
      out.println("<TR><TD>" + headerName);
      out.println("    <TD>" + request.getHeader(headerName));
    }
    out.println("</TABLE>\n</BODY></HTML>");
  }

  public void doPost(HttpServletRequest request,
                     HttpServletResponse response)
      throws ServletException, IOException {
    doGet(request, response);
  }
}
```

## Printing All Headers: Typical Netscape Result

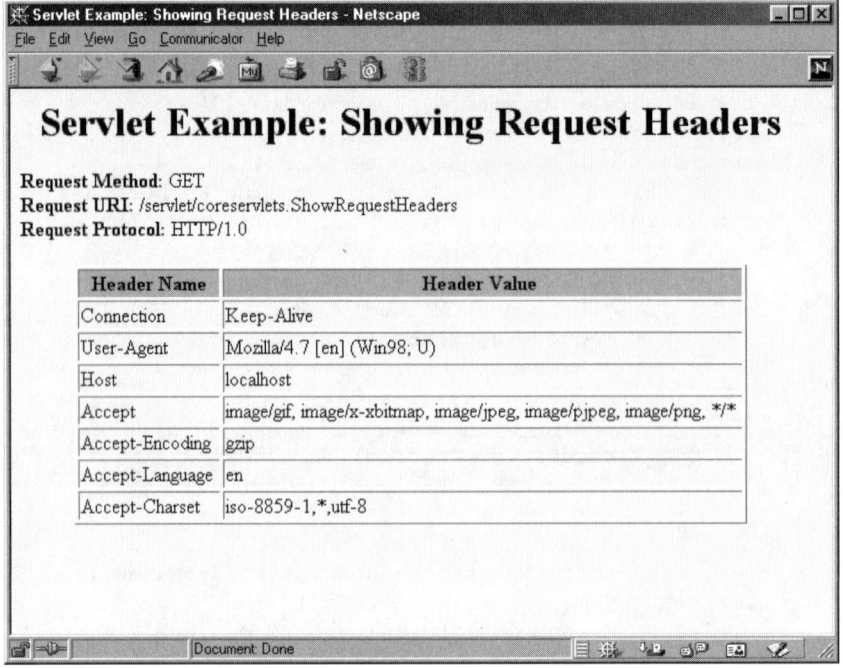

**Notes:**

# Printing All Headers: Typical Internet Explorer Result

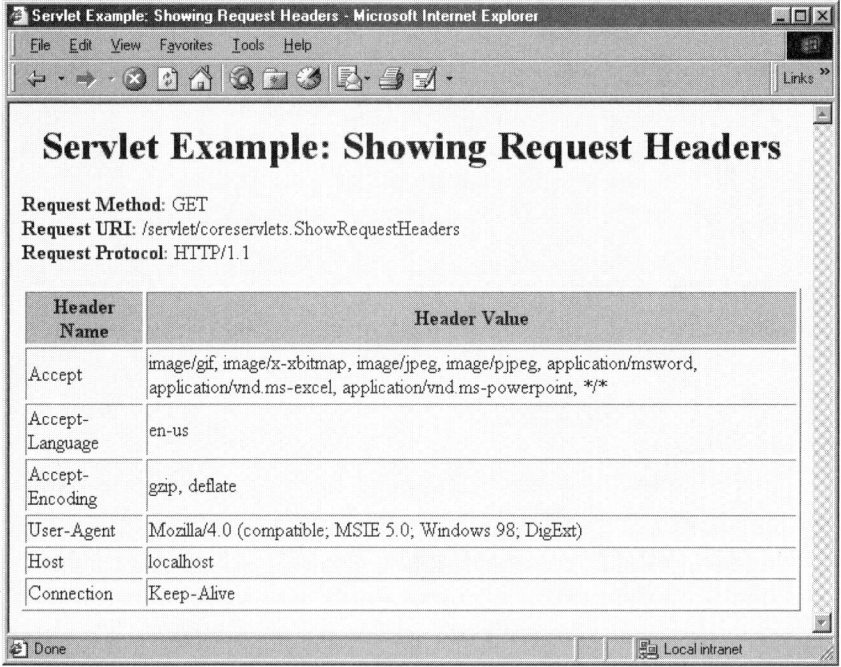

**Notes:**

## Common HTTP 1.1 Request Headers

- **Accept**
  - Indicates MIME types browser can handle.
  - Can send different content to different clients. For example, PNG files have good compression characteristics but are not widely supported in browsers. A servlet could check the Accept header to see if PNG is supported, sending <IMG SRC="picture.png" ...> if it is supported, and <IMG SRC="picture.gif" ...> if not.
- **Accept-Encoding**
  - Indicates encodings (e.g., gzip or compress) browser can handle.
  - See following example.
- **Authorization**
  - User identification for password-protected pages.
  - See upcoming example.
  - Instead of HTTP authorization, use HTML forms to send username/password and store info in session object. This approach is usually preferable because standard HTTP authorization results in a small, terse dialog box that is unfamiliar to many users.
  - Many servers have high-level way to set up password-protected pages without explicit programming in the servlets.
- **Connection**
  - In HTTP 1.0, keep-alive means browser can handle persistent connection. In HTTP 1.1, persistent connection is default. Persistent connections mean that the server can reuse the same socket for requests very close together from the same client (e.g., the images associated with a page, or cells within a framed page).
  - Servlets can't do this unilaterally; the best they can do is to give the server enough info to permit persistent connections. So, they should set Content-Length with setContentLength (using ByteArrayOutputStream to determine length of output). See example in book.

## LECTURE 3 HANDLING THE CLIENT REQUEST: HTTP REQUEST HEADERS

- **Cookie**
  - Gives cookies previously sent to client. Use getCookies, not getHeader. See chapter and later class session.
- **Host**
  - Indicates host given in original URL.
  - This is a *required* header in HTTP 1.1. This fact is important to know if you write a custom HTTP client (e.g., WebClient used in *Core Servlets and JavaServer Pages* Chapter 2) or telnet to a server and use the HTTP/1.1 version.
- **If-Modified-Since**
  - Indicates client wants page only if it has been changed after specified date.
  - Don't handle this situation directly; implement getLastModified instead. See example in *Core Servlets and JavaServer Pages* Chapter 2.
- **Referer**
  - URL of referring Web page.
  - Useful for tracking traffic; logged by many servers.
  - Can be easily spoofed, so don't let this header be your sole means of deciding (for example) how much to pay sites that show your banner ads.
- **User-Agent**
  - String identifying the browser making the request.
  - Use with extreme caution!
  - Again, can be easily spoofed.

## Sending Compressed Pages: EncodedPage.java

```
public void doGet(HttpServletRequest request,
                  HttpServletResponse response)
    throws ServletException, IOException {
  response.setContentType("text/html");
  String encodings = request.getHeader("Accept-Encoding");
  String encodeFlag = request.getParameter("encoding");
  PrintWriter out;
  String title;
  if ((encodings != null) &&
      (encodings.indexOf("gzip") != -1) &&
      !"none".equals(encodeFlag)) {
    title = "Page Encoded with GZip";
    OutputStream out1 = response.getOutputStream();
    out = new PrintWriter(new GZIPOutputStream(out1), false);
    response.setHeader("Content-Encoding", "gzip");
  } else {
    title = "Unencoded Page";
    out = response.getWriter();
  }

   out.println(ServletUtilities.headWithTitle(title) +
              "<BODY BGCOLOR=\"#FDF5E6\">\n" +
              "<H1 ALIGN=CENTER>" + title + "</H1>\n");
  String line = "Blah, blah, blah, blah, blah. " +
                "Yadda, yadda, yadda, yadda.";
  for(int i=0; i<10000; i++) {
    out.println(line);
  }
  out.println("</BODY></HTML>");
  out.close();
}
```

## Sending Compressed Pages: Results

- Uncompressed (28.8K modem), Netscape 4.7, and Internet Explorer 5.0: > 50 seconds
- Compressed (28.8K modem), Netscape 4.7, and Internet Explorer 5.0: < 5 seconds
- Caution: problems with benchmarks

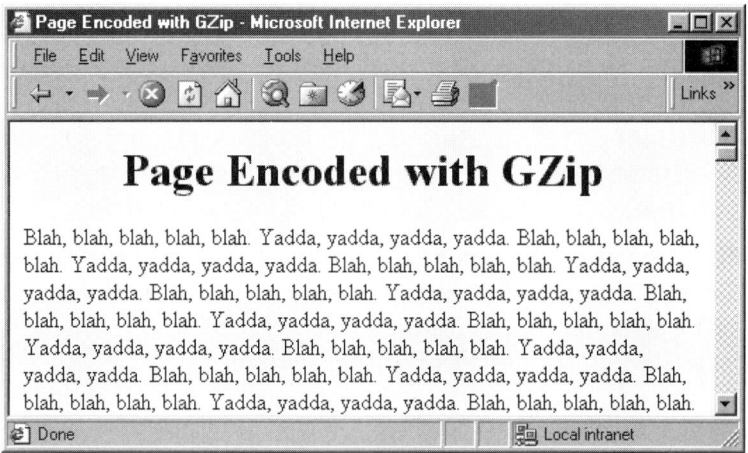

## Notes:

## Restricting Access to Web Pages

- **1st alternative: server-specific mechanisms**
- **2nd alternative: forms and sessions**
- **3rd alternative: standard HTTP security:**
    1. Check whether there is Authorization header. If not, go to Step 2. If so, skip over word "basic" and reverse the base64 encoding of the remaining part. This results in a string of the form username:password. Check the username and password against some stored set. If it matches, return the page. If not, go to Step 2.
    2. Return a 401 (Unauthorized) response code and a header of the following form:
        WWW-Authenticate: BASIC realm="some-name"
        
        This instructs browser to pop up a dialog box telling the user to enter a name and password for some-name, then to reconnect with that username and password embedded in a single base64 string inside the Authorization header.

## Notes:

## SecretServlet (Registered Name of ProtectedPage Servlet)

```java
public class ProtectedPage extends HttpServlet {
  private Properties passwords;
  private String passwordFile;

  public void init(ServletConfig config)
      throws ServletException {
    super.init(config);
    try {
      passwordFile =
        config.getInitParameter("passwordFile");
      passwords = new Properties();
      passwords.load(new FileInputStream(passwordFile));
    } catch(IOException ioe) {}
  }

  public void doGet(HttpServletRequest request,
                    HttpServletResponse response)
      throws ServletException, IOException {
    response.setContentType("text/html");
    PrintWriter out = response.getWriter();
    String authorization =
      request.getHeader("Authorization");
    if (authorization == null) {
      askForPassword(response);
    } else {
      String userInfo =
        authorization.substring(6).trim();
      BASE64Decoder decoder = new BASE64Decoder();
      String nameAndPassword =
        new String(decoder.decodeBuffer(userInfo));
      // Check name and password

  private void askForPassword
                      (HttpServletResponse response) {
    // SC_UNAUTHORIZED is 401
    response.setStatus(response.SC_UNAUTHORIZED);
    response.setHeader("WWW-Authenticate",
                       "BASIC realm=\"privileged-few\"");
  }
```

## SecretServlet in Action

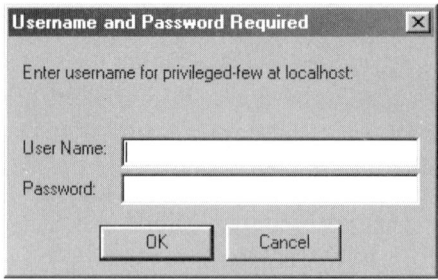

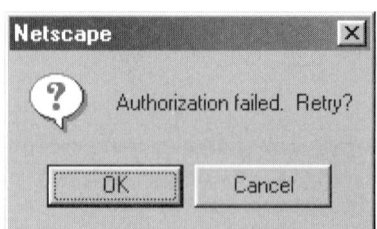

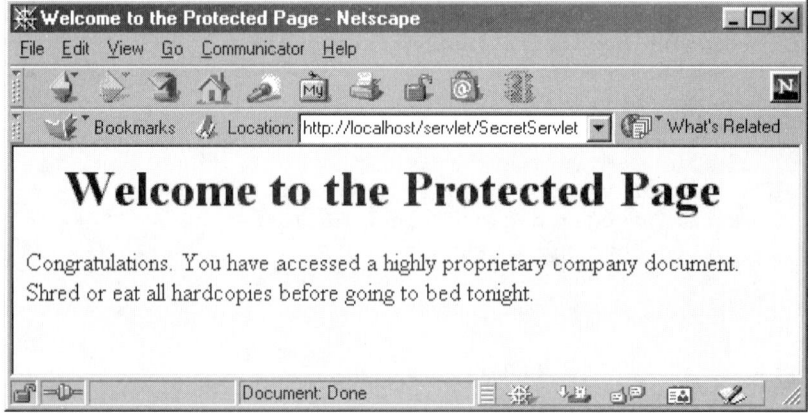

## Summary

- **Many servlet tasks can *only* be accomplished by making use of HTTP headers coming from the browser**
- **Use request.getHeader for arbitrary header**
- **Cookies, authorization info, content length, and content type have shortcut methods**
- **Most important headers you read directly**
  — Accept.
  — Accept-Encoding.
  — Connection.
  — Referer.
  — User-Agent.

## Notes:

# Lecture 4

# Generating the HTTP Response

## Agenda

- Idea of HTTP status codes
- Setting status codes from servlets
- Common HTTP 1.1 status codes
- A common front end to various Web search engines
- Idea of HTTP response headers
- Setting response headers from servlets
- Common HTTP 1.1 response headers
- Persistent servlet state and auto-reloading pages

## Notes:

## Generating the Server Response: HTTP Status Codes

- **Example HTTP 1.1 Response**
  ```
  HTTP/1.1 200 OK
  Content-Type: text/html

  <!DOCTYPE ...>
  <HTML>
  ...
  </HTML>
  ```
- **Changing the status code lets you perform a number of tasks not otherwise possible**
  — Forward client to another page.
  — Indicate a missing resource.
  — Instruct browser to use cached copy.
- **Set status *before* sending document**

### Notes:

## Setting Status Codes

- **public void setStatus(int statusCode)**
  - Use a constant for the code, not an explicit int. Constants are in HttpServletResponse.
  - Names derived from standard message. E.g., SC_OK, SC_NOT_FOUND, etc.
- **public void sendError(int code, String message)**
  - Wraps message inside small HTML document.
- **public void sendRedirect(String url)**
  - Relative URLs permitted in 2.2.
  - Sets Location header also.

## Notes:

## Common HTTP 1.1 Status Codes

- **200 (OK)**
  - Everything is fine; document follows.
  - Default for servlets.
- **204 (No Content)**
  - Browser should keep displaying previous document.
- **301 (Moved Permanently)**
  - Requested document permanently moved elsewhere (indicated in Location header).
  - Browsers go to new location automatically.
- **302 (Found)**
  - Requested document temporarily moved elsewhere (indicated in Location header).
  - Browsers go to new location automatically.
  - Servlets should use sendRedirect, not setStatus, when setting this header. See example.
- **401 (Unauthorized)**
  - Browser tried to access password-protected page without proper Authorization header. See example in book.
- **404 (Not Found)**
  - No such page. Servlets should use sendError to set this.
  - Problem: Internet Explorer 5.0.
  - Fun and games: http://www.plinko.net/404/.

## A Front End to Various Search Engines: Code

```
public void doGet(HttpServletRequest request,
                  HttpServletResponse response)
    throws ServletException, IOException {
  String searchString =
    request.getParameter("searchString");
  if ((searchString == null) ||
      (searchString.length() == 0)) {
    reportProblem(response, "Missing search string.");
    return;
  }
  searchString = URLEncoder.encode(searchString);
  String numResults =
    request.getParameter("numResults");
  ...
  String searchEngine =
    request.getParameter("searchEngine");

  SearchSpec[] commonSpecs =
   SearchSpec.getCommonSpecs();
  for(int i=0; i<commonSpecs.length; i++) {
    SearchSpec searchSpec = commonSpecs[i];
    if (searchSpec.getName().equals(searchEngine)) {
      String url =
        searchSpec.makeURL(searchString, numResults);
      response.sendRedirect(url);
      return;
    }
  }
  reportProblem(response,
                "Unrecognized search engine.");

private void reportProblem(HttpServletResponse response,
                           String message)
    throws IOException {
  response.sendError(response.SC_NOT_FOUND,
                     "<H2>" + message + "</H2>");
}
```

# LECTURE 4  GENERATING THE HTTP RESPONSE

# Front End to Search Engines: Result of Legal Request

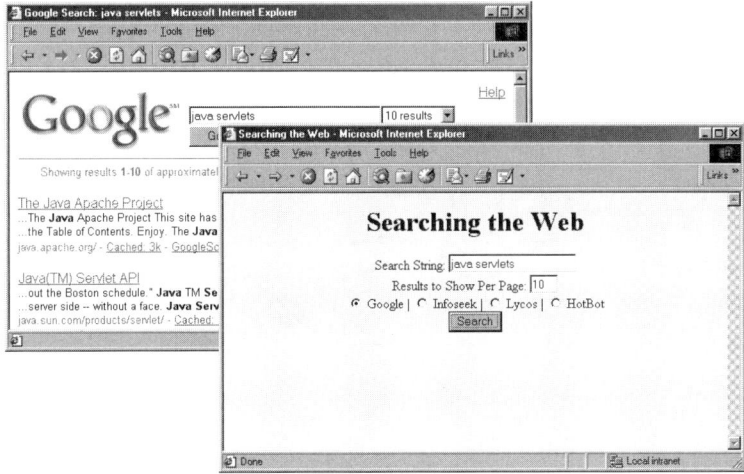

# Notes:

## Front End to Search Engines: Result of Illegal Request

- **Fix:**
  - Tools, Internet Options, deselect "Show 'friendly' HTTP error messages." Not a real fix—doesn't help unsuspecting *users* of your pages.

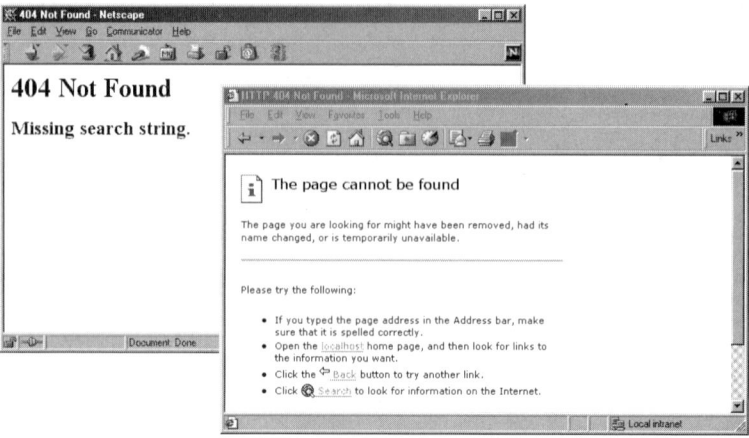

## Notes:

# LECTURE 4 GENERATING THE HTTP RESPONSE

## Generating the Server Response: HTTP Response Headers

- **Purposes**
  — Give forwarding location.
  — Specify cookies.
  — Supply the page modification date.
  — Instruct the browser to reload the page after a designated interval.
  — Give the document size so that persistent HTTP connections can be used.
  — Designate the type of document being generated.
  — Etc.

## Notes:

## Setting Arbitrary Response Headers

- **public void setHeader(String headerName, String headerValue)**
  — Sets an arbitrary header.
- **public void setDateHeader(String name, long millisecs)**
  — Converts milliseconds since 1970 to a date string in GMT format.
- **public void setIntHeader(String name, int headerValue)**
  — Prevents need to convert int to String before calling setHeader.
- **addHeader, addDateHeader, addIntHeader**
  — Adds new occurrence of header instead of replacing. Servlets 2.2 only.

**Notes:**

## Setting Common Response Headers

- **setContentType**
  — Sets the Content-Type header.
    Servlets almost always use this.
    See table of common MIME types.
- **setContentLength**
  — Sets the Content-Length header.
    Used for persistent HTTP connections.
    See Connection request header.
- **addCookie**
  — Adds a value to the Set-Cookie header.
    See separate section on cookies.
- **sendRedirect**
  — Sets the Location header (plus changes status code).

## Notes:

## Common MIME Types

| Type | Meaning |
| --- | --- |
| application/msword | Microsoft Word document |
| application/octet-stream | Unrecognized or binary data |
| application/pdf | Acrobat (.pdf) file |
| application/postscript | PostScript file |
| application/vnd.lotus-notes | Lotus Notes file |
| application/vnd.ms-excel | Excel spreadsheet |
| application/vnd.ms-powerpoint | Powerpoint presentation |
| application/x-gzip | Gzip archive |
| application/x-java-archive | JAR file |
| application/x-java-vm | Java bytecode (.class) file |
| application/zip | Zip archive |
| audio/basic | Sound file in .au or .snd format |
| audio/x-aiff | AIFF sound file |
| audio/x-wav | Microsoft Windows sound file |
| audio/midi | MIDI sound file |
| text/css | HTML cascading style sheet |
| text/html | HTML document |
| text/plain | Plain text |
| image/gif | GIF image |
| image/jpeg | JPEG image |
| image/png | PNG image |
| image/tiff | TIFF image |
| video/mpeg | MPEG video clip |
| video/quicktime | QuickTime video clip |

**Notes:**

## LECTURE 4 GENERATING THE HTTP RESPONSE

## Common HTTP 1.1 Response Headers

- **Cache-Control (1.1) and Pragma (1.0)**
  - A no-cache value prevents browsers from caching page. Send both headers or check HTTP version.
- **Content-Encoding**
  - The way document is encoded. Browser reverses this encoding before handling document. See compression example earlier.
- **Content-Length**
  - The number of bytes in the response.
  - See setContentLength on previous slide.
  - Use ByteArrayOutputStream to buffer document before sending it, so that you can determine size. See discussion of the Connection request header and detailed example in book.
- **Content-Type**
  - The MIME type of the document being returned.
  - Use setContentType to set this header.
- **Expires**
  - The time at which document should be considered out-of-date and thus should no longer be cached.
  - Use setDateHeader to set this header.
- **Last-Modified**
  - The time document was last changed.
  - Don't set this header explicitly; provide a getLastModified method instead. See example in *Core Servlets and JavaServer Pages* Chapter 2.
- **Location**
  - The URL to which browser should reconnect.
  - Use sendRedirect instead of setting this directly.
- **Refresh**
  - The number of seconds until browser should reload page. Can also include URL to connect to. See following example.
- **Set-Cookie**
  - The cookies that browser should remember. Don't set this header directly; use addCookie instead. See next section.
- **WWW-Authenticate**
  - The authorization type and realm needed in Authorization header. See example in *Core Servlets and JavaServer Pages* Section 4.5.

## Persistent Servlet State and Auto-Reloading Pages

- **Idea: generate list of large (e.g., 150-digit) prime numbers**
  — Show partial results until completed.
  — Let new clients make use of results from others.
- **Demonstrates use of the Refresh header**
- **Shows how easy it is for servlets to maintain state between requests**
  — Very difficult in traditional CGI.
- **Also illustrates that servlets can handle multiple simultaneous connections**
  — Each request is in a separate thread.

## Notes:

# Generating Prime Numbers: Source Code

```
public void doGet(HttpServletRequest request,
                  HttpServletResponse response)
    throws ServletException, IOException {
  int numPrimes =
    ServletUtilities.getIntParameter(request,
                                     "numPrimes", 50);
  int numDigits =
    ServletUtilities.getIntParameter(request,
                                     "numDigits", 120);
  // findPrimeList is synchronized
  PrimeList primeList =
    findPrimeList(primeListVector, numPrimes, numDigits);
  if (primeList == null) {
    primeList = new PrimeList(numPrimes, numDigits, true);
    synchronized(primeListVector) {
      if (primeListVector.size() >= maxPrimeLists)
        primeListVector.removeElementAt(0);
      primeListVector.addElement(primeList);
    }
  }
  Vector currentPrimes = primeList.getPrimes();
  int numCurrentPrimes = currentPrimes.size();
  int numPrimesRemaining = (numPrimes - numCurrentPrimes);
  boolean isLastResult = (numPrimesRemaining == 0);
  if (!isLastResult) {
    response.setHeader("Refresh", "5");
  }
  response.setContentType("text/html");
  PrintWriter out = response.getWriter();
  // Show List of Primes found ...
```

## Prime Number Servlet: Front End

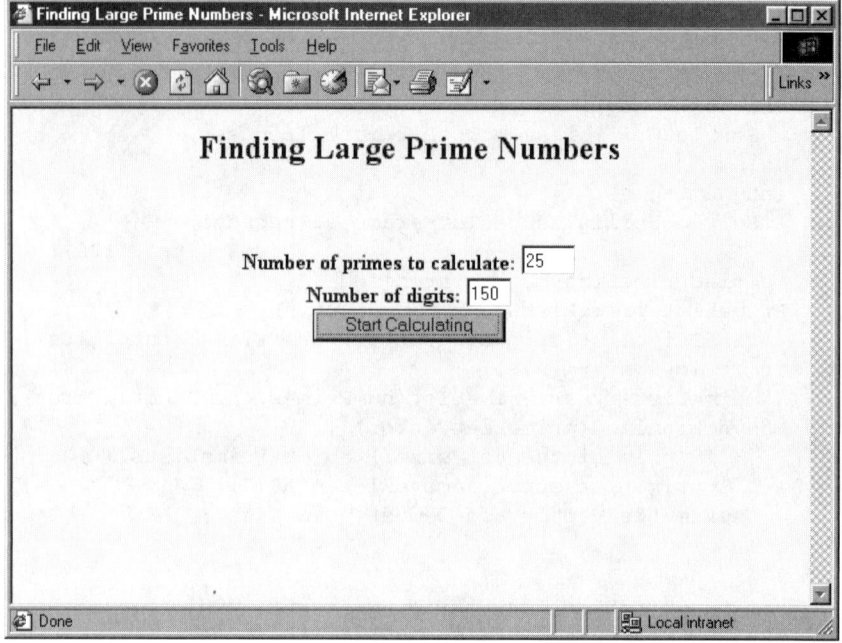

## Notes:

## LECTURE 4 GENERATING THE HTTP RESPONSE

## Prime Number Servlet: Initial Result

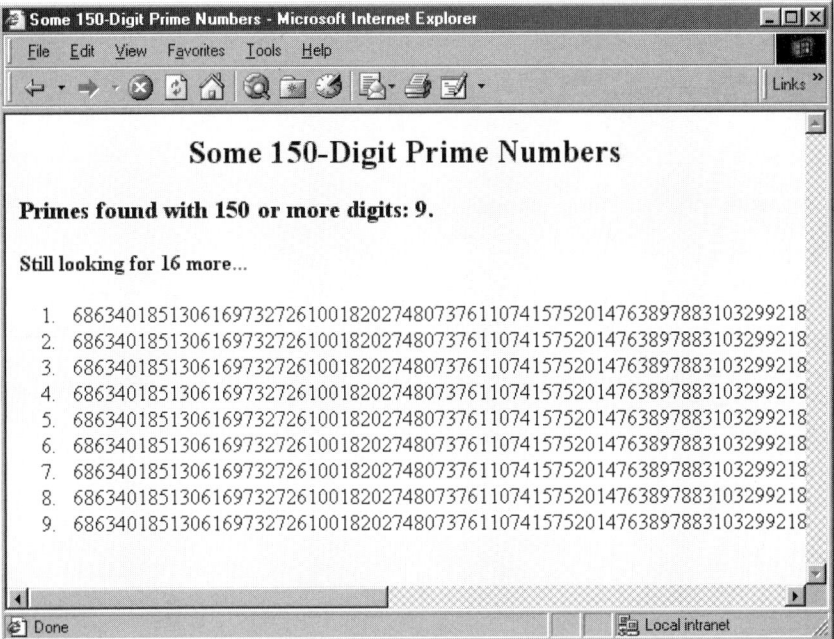

## Notes:

## Prime Number Servlet: Final Result

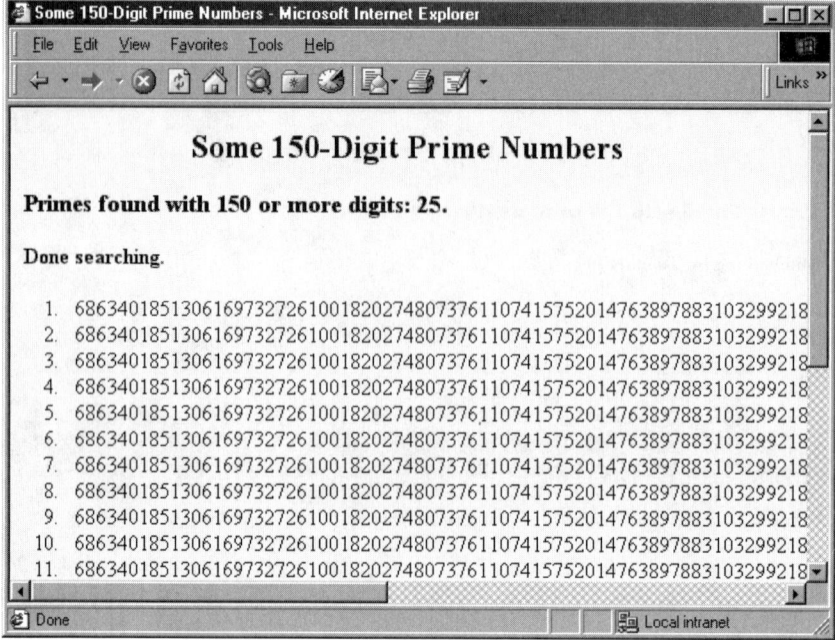

## Notes:

## Summary

- **Many servlet tasks can *only* be accomplished through use of HTTP status codes and headers sent to the browser**
- **Two parts of the response**
    — Status line.
        - In general, set via response.setStatus.
        - In special cases, set via response.sendRedirect and response.sendError.
    — Response headers.
        - In general, set via response.setHeader.
        - In special cases, set via response.setContentType, response.setContentLength, response.addCookie, and response.sendRedirect.
- **Most important status codes**
    — 200 (default).
    — 302 (forwarding; set via sendRedirect).
    — 401 (password needed).
    — 404 (not found; set via sendError).
- **Most important headers you set directly**
    — Cache-Control and Pragma.
    — Content-Encoding.
    — Content-Length.
    — Expires.
    — Refresh.
    — WWW-Authenticate.

# Lecture 5

# Handling Cookies

## Agenda

- The potential of cookies
- The problems with cookies
- Sending cookies to browser
- Reading cookies from browser
- Simple cookie-handling servlets
- Cookie utilities
- Methods in the Cookie API
- A customized search engine front end

**Notes:**

## The Potential of Cookies

- **Idea**
  - Servlet sends a simple name and value to client.
  - Client returns same name and value when it connects to same site (or same domain, depending on cookie settings).
- **Typical Uses of Cookies**
  - Identifying a user during an e-commerce session.
    - Servlets have a higher-level API for this task.
  - Avoiding username and password.
  - Customizing a site.
  - Focusing advertising.

## Notes:

**Notes:**

## Some Problems with Cookies

- **The problem is privacy, not security**
  - Servers can remember your previous actions.
  - If you give out personal information, servers can link that information to your previous actions.
  - Servers can share cookie information through use of a cooperating third party like doubleclick.net.
  - Poorly designed sites store sensitive information like credit card numbers directly in cookie.
  - JavaScript bugs let hostile sites steal cookies in older browsers.
- **Moral for servlet authors**
  - Avoid servlets that totally fail when cookies are disabled.
  - Don't put sensitive info in cookies.

## Notes:

## Sending Cookies to Browser

- **Standard approach:**
  ```
  Cookie c = new Cookie("name", "value");
  c.setMaxAge(...); // Means cookie persists on disk
  // Set other attributes.
  response.addCookie(c);
  ```
- **Simplified approach:**
  — Use LongLivedCookie class:
  ```
  public class LongLivedCookie extends Cookie {
    public static final int SECONDS_PER_YEAR =
      60*60*24*365;

    public LongLivedCookie(String name, String value) {
      super(name, value);
      setMaxAge(SECONDS_PER_YEAR);
    }
  }
  ```
- **Reminder:**
  —All code from the book and video is
    online at www.coreservlets.com.

## Notes:

## LECTURE 5 HANDLING COOKIES

## Reading Cookies from Browser

- **Standard approach:**
```
Cookie[] cookies = request.getCookies();
if (cookies != null) {
  for(int i=0; i<cookies.length; i++ {
    Cookie c = cookies[i];
    if (c.getName() .equals("someName")) {
      doSomethingWith(c);
      break;
    }
  }
}
```
- **Simplified approach:**
  — Extract cookie or cookie value from cookie array by using ServletUtilities.getCookieValue or ServletUtilities.getCookie.

## Notes:

## Simple Cookie-Setting Servlet

```
public class SetCookies extends HttpServlet {
  public void doGet(HttpServletRequest request,
                    HttpServletResponse response)
      throws ServletException, IOException {
    for(int i=0; i<3; i++) {
      Cookie cookie = new Cookie("Session-Cookie-" + i,
                                 "Cookie-Value-S" + i);
      response.addCookie(cookie);
      cookie = new Cookie("Persistent-Cookie-" + i,
                          "Cookie-Value-P" + i);
      cookie.setMaxAge(3600);
      response.addCookie(cookie);
    }
    response.setContentType("text/html");
    PrintWriter out = response.getWriter();
    out.println(...);
```

**Notes:**

## Result of Cookie-Setting Servlet

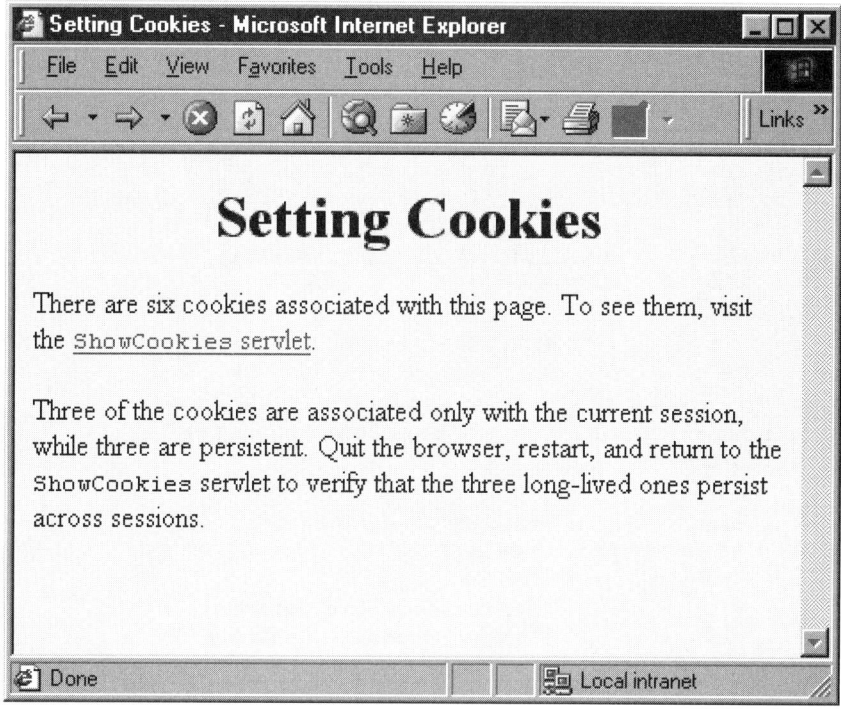

**Notes:**

## Simple Cookie-Viewing Servlet

```java
public class ShowCookies extends HttpServlet {
  public void doGet(HttpServletRequest request,
                    HttpServletResponse response)
      throws ServletException, IOException {
    response.setContentType("text/html");
    PrintWriter out = response.getWriter();
    String title = "Active Cookies";
    out.println(ServletUtilities.headWithTitle(title) +
                "<BODY BGCOLOR=\"#FDF5E6\">\n" +
                "<H1 ALIGN=\"CENTER\">" + title +
                "</H1>\n" +
                "<TABLE BORDER=1 ALIGN=\"CENTER\">\n" +
                "<TR BGCOLOR=\"#FFAD00\">\n" +
                "  <TH>Cookie Name\n" +
                "  <TH>Cookie Value");
    Cookie[] cookies = request.getCookies();
    if (cookies != null) {
      Cookie cookie;
      for(int i=0; i<cookies.length; i++) {
        cookie = cookies[i];
        out.println("<TR>\n" +
                    "  <TD>" + cookie.getName() + "\n" +
                    "  <TD>" + cookie.getValue());
      }
    }
    out.println("</TABLE></BODY></HTML>");
  }
}
```

## LECTURE 5  HANDLING COOKIES

## Result of Cookie-Viewer (Before and After Restarting Browser)

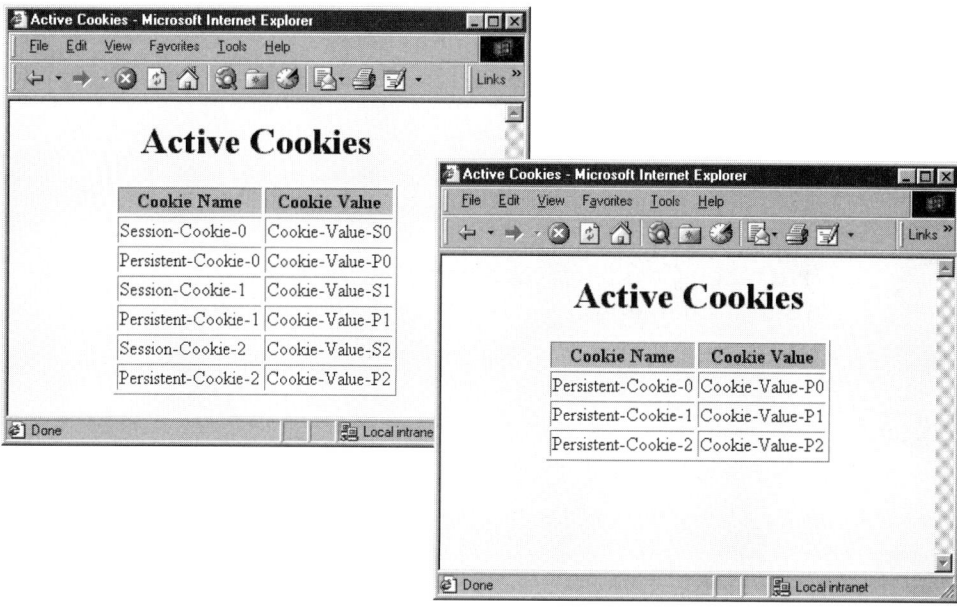

## Notes:

## Cookie Utilities

- **Problem**
  - getCookies returns an array of cookies.
  - You almost always only care about one particular cookie.
- **Solution**
  - Static methods to
    - Extract a cookie value given a cookie name (default value if no match).
    - Extract a Cookie object given a cookie name (null if no match).

## Notes:

## ServletUtilities.getCookieValue

```
public static String getCookieValue(Cookie[] cookies,
                                    String cookieName,
                                    String defaultVal) {
  if (cookies != null) {
    for(int i=0; i<cookies.length; i++) {
      Cookie cookie = cookies[i];
      if (cookieName.equals(cookie.getName()))
        return(cookie.getValue());
    }
  }
  return(defaultVal);
}
```

## Notes:

## ServletUtilities.getCookie

```java
public static Cookie getCookie(Cookie[] cookies,
                               String cookieName) {
  if (cookies != null) {
    for(int i=0; i<cookies.length; i++) {
      Cookie cookie = cookies[i];
      if (cookieName.equals(cookie.getName()))
        return(cookie);
    }
  }
  return(null);
}
```

**Notes:**

## Methods in the Cookie API

- **getDomain/setDomain**
  - Lets you specify domain to which cookie applies. Current host must be part of domain specified.
- **getMaxAge/setMaxAge**
  - Gets/sets the cookie expiration time (in seconds). If you fail to set this, cookie applies to current browsing session only. See LongLivedCookie helper class given earlier.
- **getName/setName**
  - Gets/sets the cookie name. For new cookies, you supply name to constructor, not to setName. For incoming cookie array, you use getName to find the cookie of interest.
- **getPath/setPath**
  - Gets/sets the path to which cookie applies. If unspecified, cookie applies to URLs that are within or below directory containing current page.
- **getSecure/setSecure**
  - Gets/sets flag indicating whether cookie should apply only to SSL connections or to all connections.
- **getValue/setValue**
  - Gets/sets value associated with cookie. For new cookies, you supply value to constructor, not to setValue. For incoming cookie array, you use getName to find the cookie of interest, then call getValue on the result.

## A Customized Search Engine Interface

- **Front end remembers settings for search engine, search string, and hits per page**
  - Front end *uses* cookies.
  - Back end *sets* cookies.
  - In real life, don't really show previous queries!

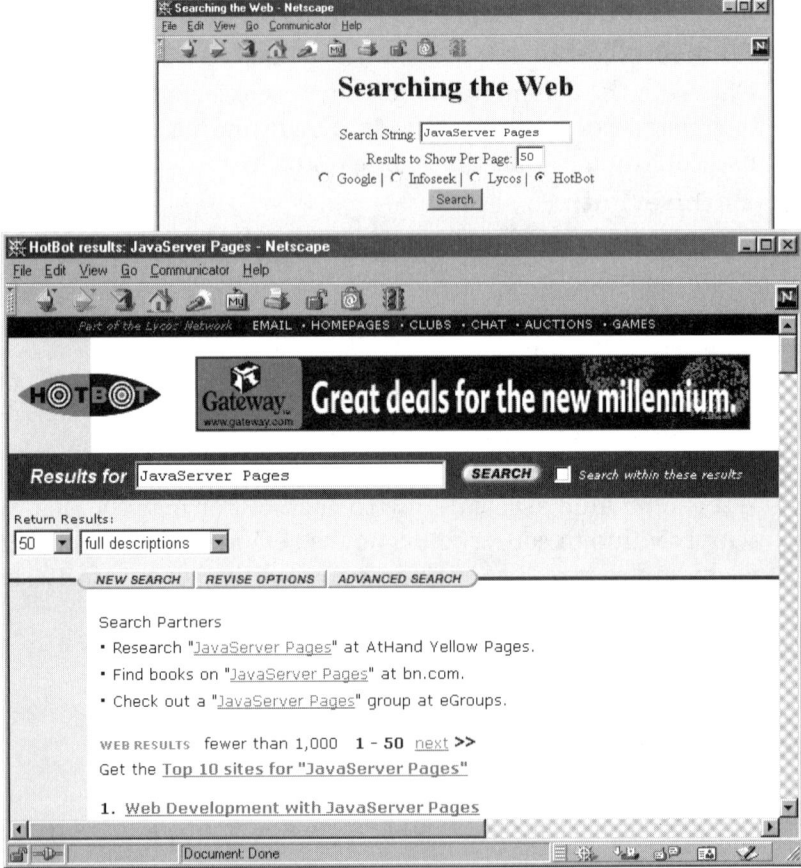

## LECTURE 5 HANDLING COOKIES

# Front End to SearchEngines Servlet

```java
public class SearchEnginesFrontEnd extends HttpServlet {
  public void doGet(HttpServletRequest request,
                    HttpServletResponse response)
      throws ServletException, IOException {
    Cookie[] cookies = request.getCookies();
    String searchString =
      ServletUtilities.getCookieValue(cookies,
                                      "searchString",
                                      "Java Programming");
    String numResults =
      ServletUtilities.getCookieValue(cookies,
                                      "numResults",
                                      "10");
    String searchEngine =
      ServletUtilities.getCookieValue(cookies,
                                      "searchEngine",
                                      "google");
    ...
    out.println
      (...
       "<FORM ACTION=\"/servlet/" +
         "coreservlets.CustomizedSearchEngines\">\n" +
       "<CENTER>\n" +
       "Search String:\n" +
       "<INPUT TYPE=\"TEXT\" NAME=\"searchString\"\n" +
       "       VALUE=\"" + searchString + "\"><BR>\n" +
       "Results to Show Per Page:\n" +
       "<INPUT TYPE=\"TEXT\" NAME=\"numResults\"\n" +
       "       VALUE=" + numResults + " SIZE=3><BR>\n" +
       "<INPUT TYPE=\"RADIO\" NAME=\"searchEngine\"\n" +
       "       VALUE=\"google\"" +
       checked("google", searchEngine) + ">\n" +
       ...);
```

## Customized SearchEngines Servlet (Back End)

```
public class CustomizedSearchEngines extends HttpServlet {
  public void doGet(HttpServletRequest request,
                    HttpServletResponse response)
      throws ServletException, IOException {
    String searchString =
      request.getParameter("searchString");
    if ((searchString == null) ||
        (searchString.length() == 0)) {
      reportProblem(response, "Missing search string.");
      return;
    }
    Cookie searchStringCookie =
      new LongLivedCookie("searchString", searchString);
    response.addCookie(searchStringCookie);
    ...
  }
}
```

## Notes:

## LECTURE 5  HANDLING COOKIES

## Summary

- **Cookies involve name/value pairs sent from server to browser and returned when the same page, site, or domain is visited later**
- **Let you**
  — Track sessions (use higher-level API).
  — Permit users to avoid logging in at low-security sites.
  — Customize sites for different users.
  — Focus content or advertising.
- **Setting cookies**
  — Call Cookie constructor, set age, call response.addCookie.
- **Reading cookies**
  — Call request.getCookies, check for null look through array for matching name, use associated value.

## Notes:

# Lecture 6

# Session Tracking

## Agenda

- The purpose of session tracking
- Rolling your own session tracking
- The session tracking API
- Per-client access counts
- Shopping carts and online stores

## Notes:

## Session Tracking and E-Commerce

- **Why session tracking?**
  - When clients at on-line store add item to their shopping cart, how does server know what's already in cart?
  - When clients decide to proceed to checkout, how can server determine which previously created cart is theirs?

## Notes:

## Rolling Your Own Session Tracking: Cookies

- **Idea: associate cookie with data on server**
  ```
  String sessionID = makeUniqueString();
  Hashtable sessionInfo = new Hashtable();
  Hashtable globalTable = findTableStoringSessions();
  globalTable.put(sessionID, sessionInfo);
  Cookie sessionCookie =
    new Cookie("JSESSIONID", sessionID);
  sessionCookie.setPath("/");
  response.addCookie(sessionCookie);
  ```
- **Still to be done**
  - Extracting cookie that stores session identifier.
  - Setting appropriate expiration time for cookie.
  - Associating the hash tables with each request.
  - Generating the unique session identifiers.

## Notes:

## LECTURE 6 SESSION TRACKING

# Rolling Your Own Session Tracking: URL-Rewriting

- **Idea**
  - Client appends some extra data on the end of each URL that identifies the session.
  - Server associates that identifier with data it has stored about that session.
  - E.g., http://host/path/file.html**;jsessionid=1234**.
- **Advantage**
  - Works even if cookies are disabled or unsupported.
- **Disadvantages**
  - Lots of tedious processing.
  - Must encode all URLs referring to own site.
  - Links from other sites and bookmarks can fail.

**Notes:**

## Rolling Your Own Session Tracking: Hidden Form Fields

- **Idea**
  ```
  <INPUT TYPE="HIDDEN" NAME="session" VALUE="...">
  ```
- **Advantage**
  — Works even if cookies are disabled or unsupported.
- **Disadvantages**
  — Lots of tedious processing.
  — **All pages must be the result of form submissions.**

**Notes:**

## The Session Tracking API

- **Session objects live on the server**
- **Automatically associated with client via cookies or URL-rewriting**
  - **Use request.getSession(true) to get either existing or new session.**
    - Behind the scenes, the system looks at cookie or URL extra info and sees if it matches the key to some previously stored session object. If so, it returns that object. If not, it creates a new one, assigns a cookie or URL info as its key, and returns that new session object.
- **Hashtable-like mechanism lets you store arbitrary objects inside session**
  - putValue (setAttribute in 2.2) stores values.
  - getValue (getAttribute in 2.2) retrieves values.

## Notes:

## Looking Up Session Information: getValue

```
HttpSession session = request.getSession(true);
ShoppingCart cart =
  (ShoppingCart)session.getValue("shoppingCart");
if (cart == null) { // No cart already in session
  cart = new ShoppingCart();
  session.putValue("shoppingCart", cart);
}
doSomethingWith(cart);
```

## Notes:

## Associating Information with a Session: putValue

```
HttpSession session = request.getSession(true);
session.putValue("referringPage",
                 request.getHeader("Referer"));
ShoppingCart cart =
  (ShoppingCart)session.getValue("previousItems");
if (cart == null) { // No cart already in session
  cart = new ShoppingCart();
  session.putValue("previousItems", cart);
}
String itemID = request.getParameter("itemID");
if (itemID != null) {
  cart.addItem(Catalog.getItem(itemID));
}
```

## Notes:

## HttpSession Methods

- **getValue [2.1], getAttribute [2.2]**
  — Extracts a previously stored value from a session object. Returns null if no value is associated with given name.
- **putValue [2.1], setAttribute [2.2]**
  — Associates a value with a name. Monitors changes: values implement HttpSessionBindingListener.
- **removeValue [2.1], removeAttribute [2.2]**
  — Removes values associated with name.
- **getValueNames [2.1], getAttributeNames [2.2]**
  — Returns names of all attributes in the session.
- **getId**
  — Returns the unique identifier.
- **isNew**
  — Determines if session is new to client (not page).
- **getCreationTime**
  — Returns time at which session was first created.
- **getLastAccessedTime**
  — Returns time at which session was last sent from client.
- **getMaxInactiveInterval, setMaxInactiveInterval**
  — Gets or sets the amount of time session should go without access before being invalidated.
- **public void invalidate()**
  — Invalidates the session and unbinds all objects associated with it.

## A Servlet Showing Per-Client Access Counts

```
public void doGet(HttpServletRequest request,
                  HttpServletResponse response)
    throws ServletException, IOException {
  response.setContentType("text/html");
  PrintWriter out = response.getWriter();
  String title = "Session Tracking Example";
  HttpSession session = request.getSession(true);
  String heading;
  Integer accessCount =
    (Integer)session.getValue("accessCount");
  if (accessCount == null) {
    accessCount = new Integer(0);
    heading = "Welcome, Newcomer";
  } else {
    heading = "Welcome Back";
    accessCount = new Integer(accessCount.intValue() + 1);
  }
  session.putValue("accessCount", accessCount);
```

## Notes:

## First Visit to ShowSession Servlet

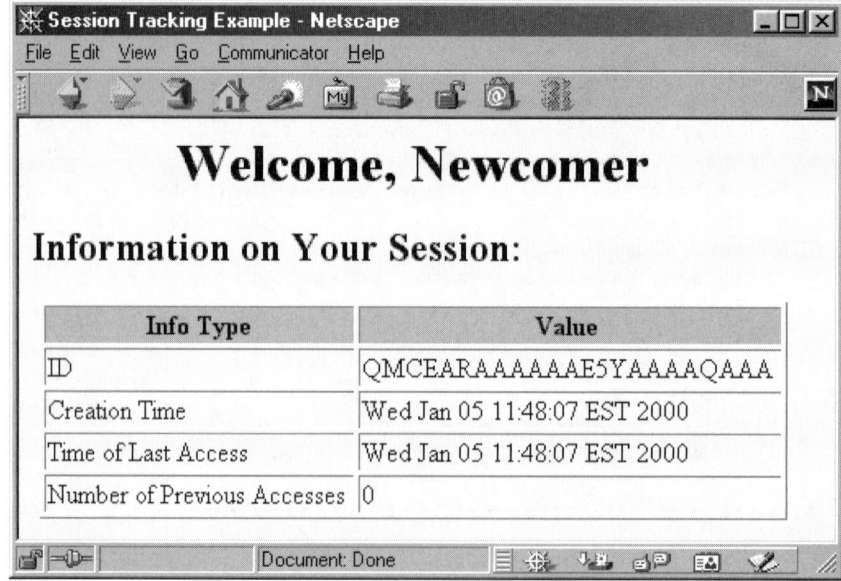

**Notes:**

## LECTURE 6  SESSION TRACKING

# Eleventh Visit to ShowSession Servlet

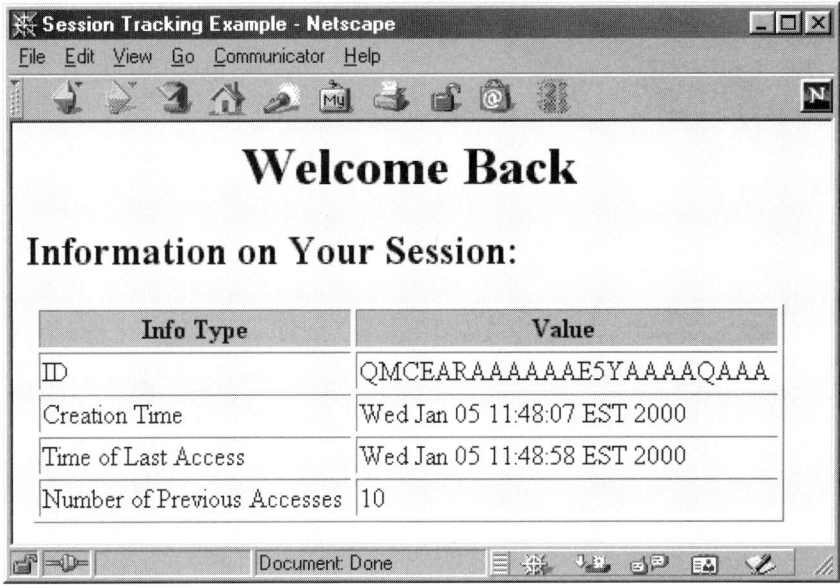

# Notes:

## Session Tracking and Shopping Carts

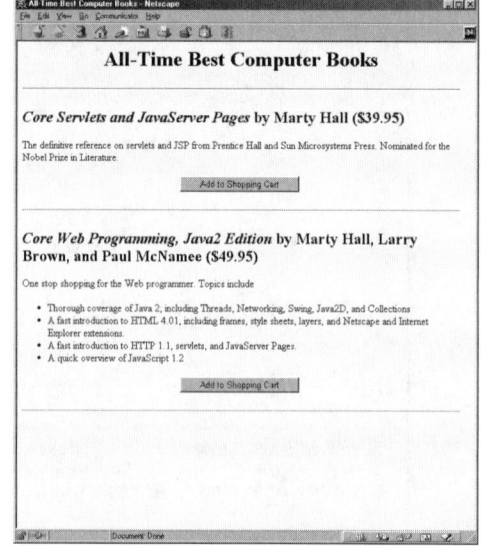
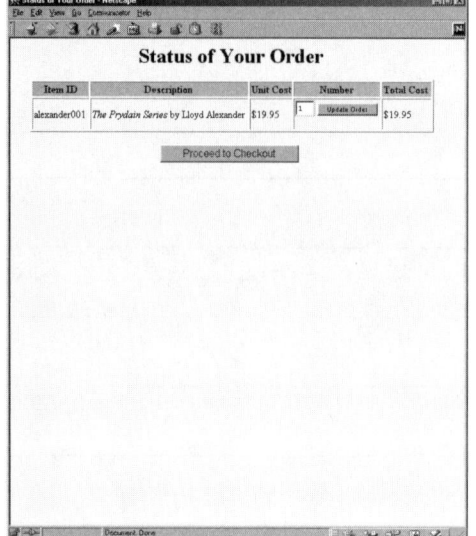
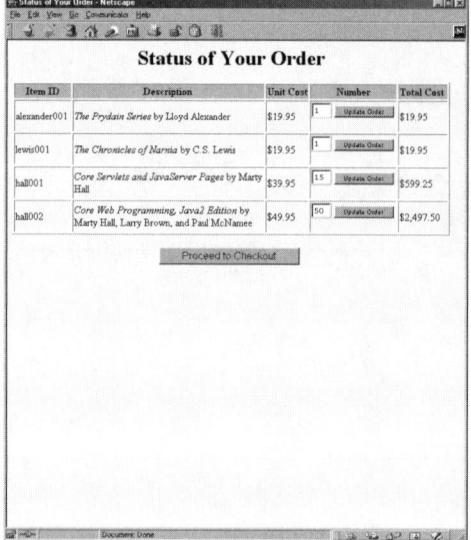

## Session Tracking and Shopping Carts (Code)

```
  cart = (ShoppingCart)session.getValue("shoppingCart");
  if (cart == null) {
    // New visitors get a fresh shopping cart.
    // Previous visitors keep using their existing cart.
    cart = new ShoppingCart();
    session.putValue("shoppingCart", cart);
  }
  String itemID = request.getParameter("itemID");
  if (itemID != null) {
    String numItemsString =
      request.getParameter("numItems");
    if (numItemsString == null) {
      // If request specified an ID but no number,
      // then customers came here via an "Add Item to Cart"
      // button on a catalog page.
      cart.addItem(itemID);
    }
    else {
      // If request specified an ID and number, then
      // customers came here via an "Update Order" button
      // after changing the number of items in order.
      // Note that specifying a number of 0 results
      // in item being deleted from cart.
      int numItems;
      try {
        numItems = Integer.parseInt(numItemsString);
      } catch(NumberFormatException nfe) {
        numItems = 1;
      }
      cart.setNumOrdered(itemID, numItems);
    }
  }
```

## Summary

- **Although it usually uses cookies behind the scenes, the session tracking API is higher-level and easier to use than the cookie API**
- **Session information lives on server**
  — Cookie or extra URL info associates it with a user.
- **Obtaining session**
  — request.getSession(true).
- **Associating values with keys**
  — session.putValue (or session.setAttribute).
- **Finding values associated with keys**
  — session.getValue (or session.getAttribute).
    - Always check if this value is null before trying to use it.

## Notes:

# Lecture 7

# Introducing JavaServer Pages

## Agenda

- Why we need JSP
- How JSP works
- Benefits of JSP
- Setting up your environment for JSP
- A simple example

## Notes:

## LECTURE 7 INTRODUCING JAVASERVER PAGES

## The Need for JSP

- **With servlets, it is easy to**
  - Read form data.
  - Read HTTP request headers.
  - Set HTTP status codes and response headers.
  - Use cookies and session tracking.
  - Share data among servlets.
  - Remember data between requests.
  - Get fun, high-paying jobs.
- **But, it sure is a pain to**
  - Use those println statements to generate HTML.
  - Maintain that HTML.

## Notes:

## The JSP Framework

- **Idea**
  - Use regular HTML for most of page.
  - Mark servlet code with special tags.
  - Entire JSP page gets translated into a servlet (once), and servlet is what actually gets invoked (for each request).
- **Example**
  - JSP.
    - Thanks for ordering
      `<I><%= request.getParameter("title") %></I>`
  - URL.
    - http://host/OrderConfirmation.jsp?title=Core+Web+Programming.
  - Result.
    - Thanks for ordering *Core Web Programming*.

## Notes:

## Benefits of JSP

- **Although JSP technically can't do anything servlets can't do, JSP makes it easier to**
  — Write HTML.
  — Read and maintain the HTML.
- **JSP makes it possible to**
  — Use standard HTML tools such as HomeSite or Dreamweaver.
  — Have different members of your team do the HTML layout than do the Java programming.
- **JSP encourages you to**
  — Separate the (Java) code that creates the content from the (HTML) code that presents it.

## Notes:

## Advantages of JSP Over Competing Technologies

- **Versus ASP or ColdFusion**
  - Better language for dynamic part.
  - Portable to multiple servers and operating systems.
- **Versus PHP**
  - Better language for dynamic part.
  - Better tool support.
- **Versus pure servlets**
  - More convenient to create HTML.
  - Can use standard tools (e.g., HomeSite).
  - Divide and conquer.
  - **JSP programmers still need to know servlet programming.**
- **Versus SSI**
  - Much more flexible and powerful.
- **Versus client-side JavaScript**
  - Many capabilities only available on server.
  - Richer language.
- **Versus server-side JavaScript**
  - Richer language.
- **Versus static HTML**
  - Dynamic features.
  - Adding dynamic features no longer "all or nothing" decision.

## Setting Up Your Environment

- **Set your CLASSPATH.** *Not.*
- **Compile your code.** *Not.*
- **Use packages to avoid name conflicts.** *Not.*
- **Put JSP page in special directory.** *Not.*
  - With Tomcat 3, HTML and JSP pages go in install_dir\webapps\ROOT\ (e.g., C:\jakarta-tomcat\webapps\ROOT\).
  - Some servers reserve certain parts of Web hierarchy for JSP pages. Tomcat 3 (standalone) doesn't.
- **Use special URL to invoke JSP page.** *Not.*
- **Caveats**
  - Previous rules about CLASSPATH, install dirs, etc., still apply to regular Java classes used by a JSP page.

## Notes:

## Example

```
<!DOCTYPE HTML PUBLIC
          "-//W3C//DTD HTML 4.0 Transitional//EN">
<HTML>
<HEAD>
<TITLE>JSP Expressions</TITLE>
<META NAME="author" CONTENT="Marty Hall">
<META NAME="keywords"
    CONTENT="JSP,expressions,JavaServer,Pages,servlets">
<META NAME="description"
      CONTENT="A quick example of JSP expressions.">
<LINK REL=STYLESHEET
      HREF="JSP-Styles.css"
      TYPE="text/css">
</HEAD>

<BODY>
<H2>JSP Expressions</H2>
<UL>
  <LI>Current time: <%= new java.util.Date() %>
  <LI>Your hostname: <%= request.getRemoteHost() %>
  <LI>Your session ID: <%= session.getId() %>
  <LI>The <CODE>testParam</CODE> form parameter:
      <%= request.getParameter("testParam") %>
</UL>
</BODY>
</HTML>
```

## Notes:

# LECTURE 7 INTRODUCING JAVASERVER PAGES

## Example Result

- **With class setup, if location was**
  - C:\jakarta-tomcat\webapps\ROOT\Expressions.jsp.
- **URL would be**
  - http://localhost/Expressions.jsp.

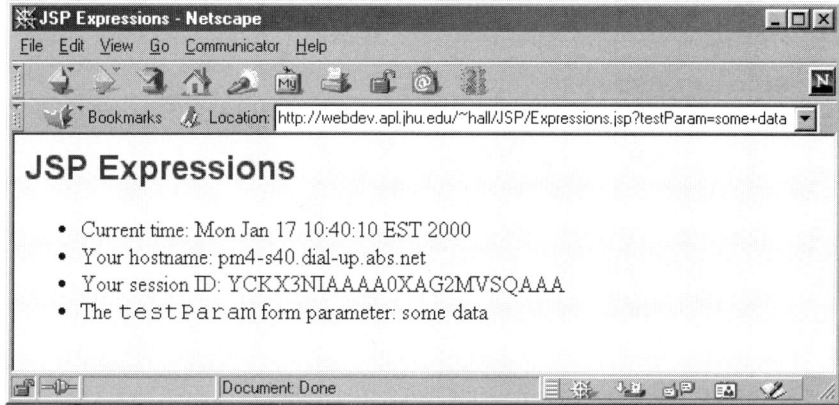

## Notes:

## Most Common Misunderstanding: Forgetting JSP is Server-Side Technology

- **Very common question**
  - I can't do such and such with HTML. Will JSP let me do it?
- **Why doesn't this question make sense?**
  - JSP runs entirely on server.
  - It doesn't change content the client (browser) can handle.
- **Similar questions**
  - How do I put a normal applet in a JSP page?
    Answer: send an <APPLET...> tag to the client.
  - How do I put an image in a JSP page?
    Answer: send an <IMG ...> tag to the client.
  - How do I use JavaScript/Acrobat/Shockwave/Etc.?
    Answer: send the appropriate HTML tags.

**Notes:**

## 2nd Most Common Misunderstanding: Translation/Request Time Confusion

- **What happens at page translation time?**
  — JSP constructs get translated into servlet code.
- **What happens at request time?**
  — Servlet code gets executed. *No* interpretation of JSP occurs at request time. The original JSP page is totally ignored at request time; only the servlet that resulted from it is used.
- **When does page translation occur?**
  — Typically, the first time JSP page is accessed after it is modified. This should never happen to real user (developers should test all JSP pages they install).
  — Page translation does *not* occur for each request.

## Notes:

**Notes:**

# LECTURE 7  INTRODUCING JAVASERVER PAGES

**Notes:**

**Notes:**

# LECTURE 7  INTRODUCING JAVASERVER PAGES

**Notes:**

**Notes:**

## Summary

- **JSP makes it easier to create and maintain HTML, while still providing full access to servlet code**
- **JSP pages get translated into servlets**
  - It is the servlets that run at request time.
  - Client does not see *anything* JSP-related.
- **You still need to understand servlets**
  - Understanding how JSP really works.
  - Servlet code called from JSP.
  - Mixing servlets and JSP.
- **Other technologies use similar approach, but aren't as portable and don't let you use Java for the "real code"**

## Notes:

# Lecture 8

# JSP Scripting Elements

## Agenda

- Basic syntax
- Types of JSP scripting elements
- Expressions
- Predefined variables
- Scriptlets
- Declarations

## Notes:

# LECTURE 8 JSP SCRIPTING ELEMENTS

## Uses of JSP Constructs

Simple Application
↓
Complex Application

- *Scripting elements calling servlet code directly*
- *Scripting elements calling servlet code indirectly (by means of utility classes)*
- Beans
- Custom tags
- Servlet/JSP combo (with beans)

Notes:

## Basic Syntax

- **HTML Text**
  - \<H1\>Blah\</H1\>
  - Passed through to client. Really turned into servlet code that looks like
    - out.println("\<H1\>Blah\</H1\>");
- **HTML Comments**
  - \<!-- Comment --\>
  - Same as other HTML: passed through to client.
- **JSP Comments**
  - <%-- Comment --%>
  - Not sent to client.
- **To get <% in output, use <\%**

## Notes:

## Types of Scripting Elements

- **Expressions**
  - Format: **<%= expression %>**
  - Evaluated and inserted into the servlet's output. I.e., results in something like out.println(expression).
- **Scriptlets**
  - Format: **<% code %>**
  - Inserted verbatim into the servlet's _jspService method (called by service).
- **Declarations**
  - Format: **<%! code %>**
  - Inserted verbatim into the body of the servlet class, outside of any existing methods.

## Notes:

## JSP Expressions

- **Format**
  - <%= Java Expression %>
- **Result**
  - Expression evaluated, converted to String, and placed into HTML page at the place it occurred in JSP page.
- **Examples**
  - Current time: <%= new java.util.Date() %>
  - Your hostname: <%= request.getRemoteHost() %>
- **XML-compatible syntax**
  - **<jsp:expression>**Java Expression**</jsp:expression>**

## Notes:

## Predefined Variables

- **request**
  — The HttpServletRequest (1st argument to service/doGet).
- **response**
  — The HttpServletResponse (2nd arg to service/doGet).
- **out**
  — The Writer (a buffered version of type JspWriter) used to send output to the client.
- **session**
  — The HttpSession associated with the request (unless disabled with the session attribute of the page directive).
- **application**
  — The ServletContext (for sharing data) as obtained via getServletConfig().getContext().

## Notes:

## JSP/Servlet Correspondence

- **Original JSP**

```
<H1>A Random Number</H1>
<%= Math.random() %>
```

- **Possible resulting servlet code**

```java
public void _jspService(HttpServletRequest request,
                        HttpServletResponse response)
    throws ServletException, IOException {
  request.setContentType("text/html");
  HttpSession session = request.getSession(true);
  JspWriter out = response.getWriter();
  out.println("<H1>A Random Number</H1>");
  out.println(Math.random());
  ...
}
```

## Notes:

## LECTURE 8 JSP SCRIPTING ELEMENTS

## Example Using JSP Expressions

```
<BODY>
<H2>JSP Expressions</H2>
<UL>
  <LI>Current time: <%= new java.util.Date() %>
  <LI>Your hostname: <%= request.getRemoteHost() %>
  <LI>Your session ID: <%= session.getId() %>
  <LI>The <CODE>testParam</CODE> form parameter:
      <%= request.getParameter("testParam") %>
</UL>
</BODY>
```

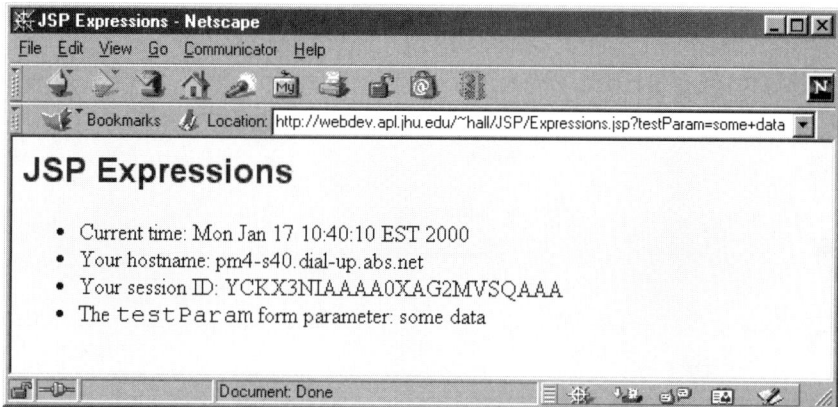

## Notes:

## JSP Scriptlets

- **Format**
  - <% Java Code %>
- **Result**
  - Code is inserted verbatim into servlet's _jspService.
- **Example**
  - <%
    String queryData = request.getQueryString();
    out.println("Attached GET data: " + queryData);
    %>
  - <% response.setContentType("text/plain"); %>
- **XML-compatible syntax**
  - **<jsp:scriptlet>**Java Code**</jsp:scriptlet>**

## Notes:

## LECTURE 8  JSP SCRIPTING ELEMENTS

## JSP/Servlet Correspondence

- **Original JSP**
  ```
  <%= foo() %>
  <% bar(); %>
  ```
- **Possible resulting servlet code**
  ```
  public void _jspService(HttpServletRequest request,
                          HttpServletResponse response)
      throws ServletException, IOException {
    request.setContentType("text/html");
    HttpSession session = request.getSession(true);
    JspWriter out = response.getWriter();
    out.println(foo());
    bar();
    ...
  }
  ```

## Notes:

## Example Using JSP Scriptlets

```
<!DOCTYPE HTML PUBLIC
          "-//W3C//DTD HTML 4.0 Transitional//EN">
<HTML>
<HEAD>
  <TITLE>Color Testing</TITLE>
</HEAD>
<%
String bgColor = request.getParameter("bgColor");
boolean hasExplicitColor;
if (bgColor != null) {
  hasExplicitColor = true;
} else {
  hasExplicitColor = false;
  bgColor = "WHITE";
}
%>

<BODY BGCOLOR="<%= bgColor %>">
<H2 ALIGN="CENTER">Color Testing</H2>
<%
if (hasExplicitColor) {
  out.println("You supplied an explicit background color of "+
              bgColor + ".");
} else {
  out.println("Using default background color of WHITE. " +
              "Supply the bgColor request attribute to try " +
              "a standard color, an RRGGBB value, or to see "+
              "if your browser supports X11 color names.");
}
%>

</BODY>
</HTML>
```

## LECTURE 8  JSP SCRIPTING ELEMENTS

# JSP Scriptlets: Results

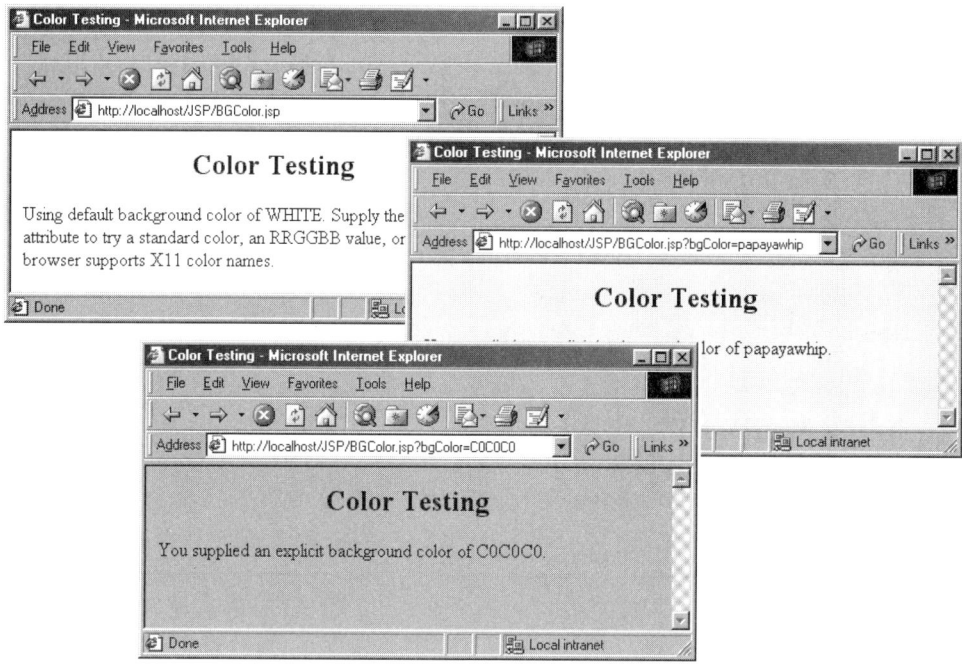

## Notes:

## Using Scriptlets to Make Parts of the JSP File Conditional

- **Point**
  - Scriptlets are inserted into servlet exactly as written.
  - Need not be complete Java expressions.
  - Complete expressions are usually clearer and easier to maintain, however.
- **Example**
  - ```
    <% if (Math.random() < 0.5) { %>
      Have a <B>nice</B> day!
    <% } else { %>
      Have a <B>lousy</B> day!
    <% } %>
    ```
- **Representative result**
  - ```
    if (Math.random() < 0.5) {
      out.println("Have a <B>nice</B> day!");
    } else {
      out.println("Have a <B>lousy</B> day!");
    }
    ```

## Notes:

## JSP Declarations

- **Format**
  — <%! Java Code %>
- **Result**
  — Code is inserted verbatim into servlet's class definition, outside of any existing methods.
- **Examples**
  — <%! private int someField = 5; %>
  — <%! private void someMethod(...) {...} %>
- **XML-compatible syntax**
  — <jsp:declaration>Java Code</jsp:declaration>

## Notes:

## JSP/Servlet Correspondence

- **Original JSP**

```
<H1>Some Heading</H1>
<%!
  public String randomHeading() {
    return("<H2>" + Math.random() + "</H2>");
  }
%>
<%= randomHeading() %>
```

## Notes:

## LECTURE 8  JSP SCRIPTING ELEMENTS

## JSP/Servlet Correspondence

- **Possible resulting servlet code**

```
public class xxxx extends HttpServlet {
 public String randomHeading() {
   return("<H2>" + Math.random() + "</H2>");
 }

 public void _jspService(HttpServletRequest request,
                         HttpServletResponse response)
     throws ServletException, IOException {
   request.setContentType("text/html");
   HttpSession session = request.getSession(true);
   JspWriter out = response.getWriter();
   out.println(<H1>Some Heading</H1>);
   out.println(randomHeading());
   ...
 }
```

## Notes:

## Example Using JSP Declarations

```html
<!DOCTYPE HTML PUBLIC
        "-//W3C//DTD HTML 4.0 Transitional//EN">
<HTML><HEAD><TITLE>JSP Declarations</TITLE>
<LINK REL=STYLESHEET
      HREF="JSP-Styles.css"
      TYPE="text/css">
</HEAD>

<BODY>
<H1>JSP Declarations</H1>

<%! private int accessCount = 0; %>
<H2>Accesses to page since server reboot:
<%= ++accessCount %></H2>

</BODY>
</HTML>
```

## Notes:

# LECTURE 8 JSP SCRIPTING ELEMENTS

## JSP Declarations: Result

- **After 15 total visits by an arbitrary number of different clients**

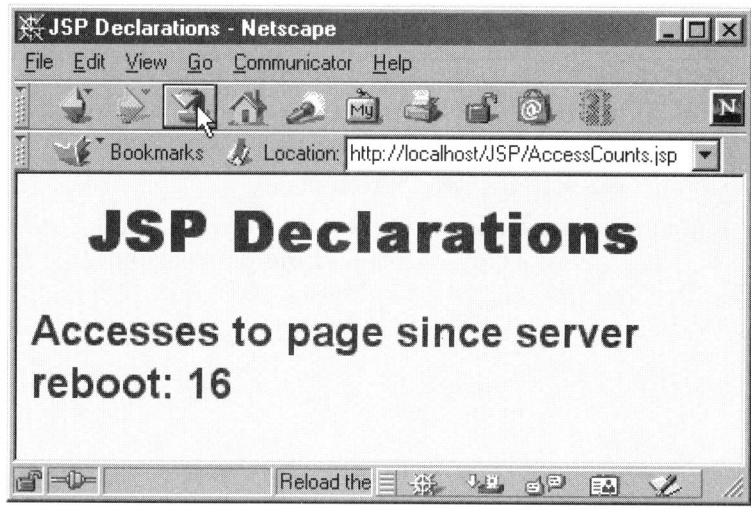

## Notes:

## JSP Declarations: the jspInit and jspDestroy Methods

- **JSP pages, like regular servlets, sometimes want to use init and destroy**
- **Problem: the servlet that gets built from the JSP page might already use init and destroy**
  - Overriding them would cause problems.
  - Thus, it is illegal to use JSP declarations to declare init or destroy.
- **Solution: use jspInit and jspDestroy**
  - The auto-generated servlet is guaranteed to call these methods from init and destroy, but the standard versions of jspInit and jspDestroy are empty (placeholders for you to override).

**Notes:**

## JSP Declarations and Predefined Variables

- **Problem**
  - The predefined variables (request, response, out, session, etc.) are *local* to the _jspService method. Thus, they are not available to methods defined by JSP declarations or to methods in helper classes. What can you do about this?
- **Solution: pass them as arguments. E.g.,**
  ```
  <%!
  public void someMethod(HttpSession s) {
    doSomethingWith(s);
  }
  %>
  <% someMethod(session); %>
  ```
- **Note that the println method of JspWriter throws IOException**
  - Use "throws IOException" for methods that use println.

**Notes:**

## Using JSP Expressions as Attribute Values

- **Static Value**
  ```
  <jsp:setProperty
    name="author"
    property="firstName"
    value="Marty" />
  ```
- **Dynamic Value**
  ```
  <jsp:setProperty
    name="user"
    property="id"
    value='<%= "UserID" + Math.random() %>' />
  ```

## Notes:

## LECTURE 8 JSP SCRIPTING ELEMENTS

## Attributes That Permit JSP Expressions

- **The name and value properties of jsp:setProperty**
  — See upcoming section on beans.
- **The page attribute of jsp:include**
  — See upcoming section on including files and applets.
- **The page attribute of jsp:forward**
  — See upcoming section on integrating servlets and JSP.
- **The value attribute of jsp:param**
  — See upcoming section on including files and applets.

## Notes:

## Summary

- **JSP Expressions**
  - Format: <%= expression %>
  - Evaluated and inserted into the servlet's output.
- **JSP Scriptlets**
  - Format: <% code %>
  - Inserted verbatim into the servlet's _jspService method.
- **JSP Declarations**
  - Format: <%! code %>
  - Inserted verbatim into the body of the servlet class.
- **Predefined variables**
  - request, response, out, session, application.
- **Limit the Java code that is directly in page**
  - Use helper classes, beans, custom tags, servlet/JSP combo.

## Notes:

# Lecture 9

# The JSP Page Directive: Structuring Generated Servlets

## Agenda

- The import attribute
- The contentType attribute
- Generating plain text and Excel documents
- The isThreadSafe attribute
- The session attribute
- The buffer attribute
- The autoflush attribute
- The extends attribute
- The errorPage attribute
- The isErrorPage attribute

## Notes:

## LECTURE 9 THE JSP PAGE DIRECTIVE

## Purpose of the page Directive

- **Give high-level information about the servlet that will result from the JSP page**
- **Can control**
  — Which classes are imported.
  — What class the servlet extends.
  — What MIME type is generated.
  — How multithreading is handled.
  — If the servlet participates in sessions.
  — The size and behavior of the output buffer.
  — What page handles unexpected errors.

## Notes:

## The import Attribute

- **Format**
    - <%@ page import="package.class" %>
    - <%@ page import="package.class1,...,package.classN" %>
- **Purpose**
    - Generate import statements at top of servlet definition.
- **Notes**
    - Although JSP pages can be almost anywhere on server, classes used by JSP pages must be in normal servlet dirs.
    - For class setup with Tomcat 3.1, this is C:\jakarta-tomcat\webapps\ROOT\WEB-INF\classes or ...\ROOT\WEB-INF\classes\directoryMatchingPackage.
    - XML-compatible syntax:
        - <jsp:directive.*directiveType* attribute="value" />

## Notes:

## Example of import Attribute

```jsp
...
<BODY>
<H2>The import Attribute</H2>
<%-- JSP page directive --%>
<%@ page import="java.util.*,coreservlets.*" %>

<%-- JSP Declaration --%>
<%!
private String randomID() {
  int num = (int)(Math.random()*10000000.0);
  return("id" + num);
}

private final String NO_VALUE = "<I>No Value</I>";
%>
<%-- JSP Scriptlet --%>
<%
Cookie[] cookies = request.getCookies();
String oldID =
  ServletUtilities.getCookieValue(cookies, "userID", NO_VALUE);
String newID;
if (oldID.equals(NO_VALUE)) {
  newID = randomID();
} else {
  newID = oldID;
}
LongLivedCookie cookie = new LongLivedCookie("userID", newID);
response.addCookie(cookie);
%>
<%-- JSP Expressions --%>
This page was accessed at <%= new Date() %> with a userID
cookie of <%= oldID %>.
 </BODY></HTML>
```

## Example of import Attribute: Result

- **First access**

- **Subsequent accesses**

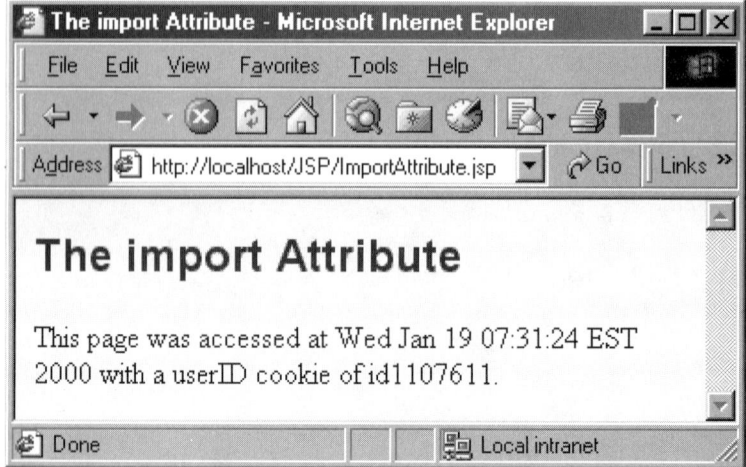

## The contentType Attribute

- **Format**
  - <%@ page contentType="MIME-Type" %>
  - <%@ page contentType="MIME-Type; charset=Character-Set" %>
- **Purpose**
  - Specify the MIME type of the page generated by the servlet that results from the JSP page.
- **Notes**
  - Attribute value cannot be computed at request time.
  - See section on response headers for table of the most common MIME types.

## Notes:

## Using contentType to Generate Plain Text Documents

```
<!DOCTYPE HTML PUBLIC
          "-//W3C//DTD HTML 4.0 Transitional//EN">
<HTML>
<HEAD>
<TITLE>The contentType Attribute</TITLE>
</HEAD>
<BODY>

<H2>The contentType Attribute</H2>
<%@ page contentType="text/plain" %>
This should be rendered as plain text,
<B>not</B> as HTML.

</BODY>
</HTML>
```

## Notes:

## LECTURE 9 THE JSP PAGE DIRECTIVE

# Plain Text Documents in Netscape (Correct)

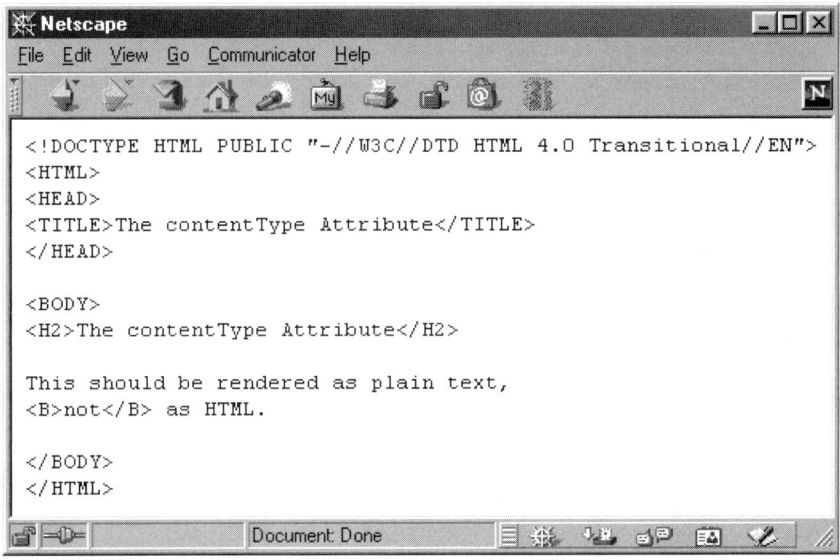

# Notes:

## Plain Text Documents in Internet Explorer (Incorrect)

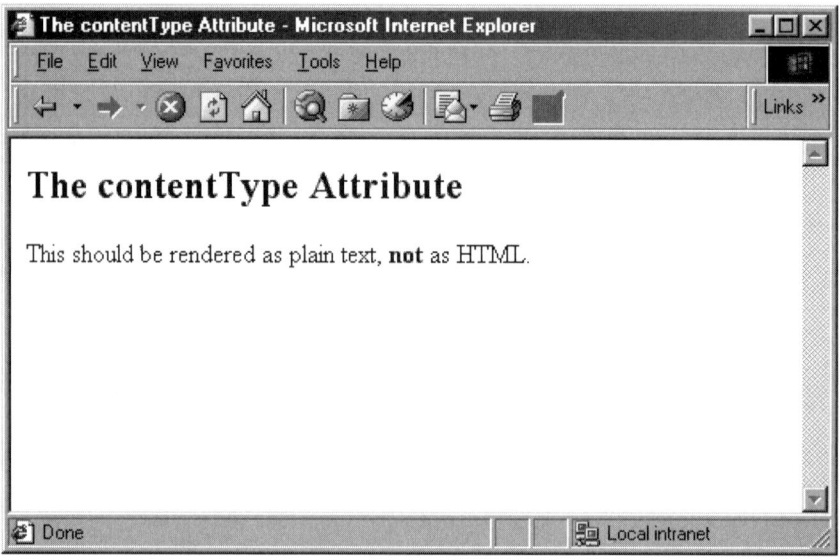

## Notes:

## LECTURE 9 THE JSP PAGE DIRECTIVE

## Generating Excel Spreadsheets

```
<%@ page contentType="application/vnd.ms-excel" %>
<%-- Note that there are tabs,
   not spaces, between columns. --%>
1997	1998	1999	2000	2001 (Anticipated)
12.3	13.4	14.5	15.6	16.7
```

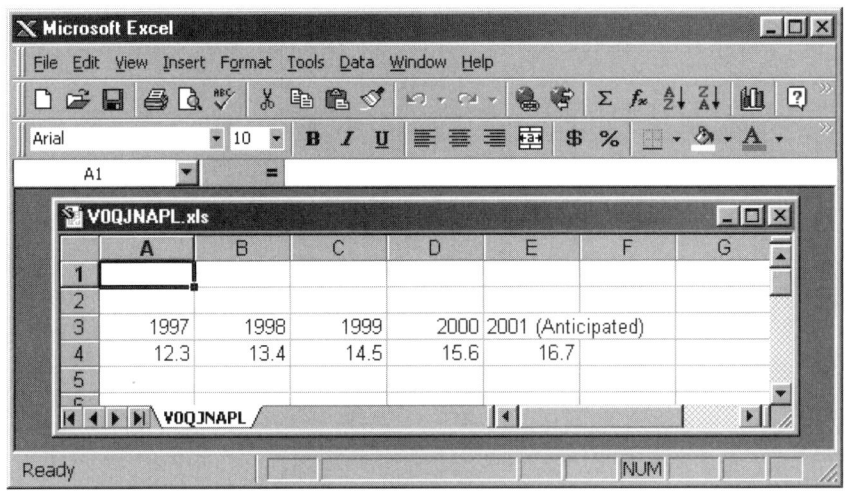

## Notes:

## Generating Excel Spreadsheets Conditionally

- **Excel can interpret HTML tables**
  — Change MIME type based on request parameters.
- **You cannot use page directive**
  — It does not use request-time values.
- **Solution**
  — Use predefined request variable and call setContentType.
  ```
  <%
  if (someCondition) {
    response.setContentType("type1");
  } else {
    response.setContentType("type2");
  }
  %>
  ```

## Notes:

## Generating Excel Spreadsheets Conditionally

```
<!DOCTYPE ...>
<HTML><HEAD>
<TITLE>Comparing Apples and Oranges</TITLE>
<LINK REL=STYLESHEET
      HREF="JSP-Styles.css"
      TYPE="text/css">
</HEAD>
<BODY>
<CENTER>
<H2>Comparing Apples and Oranges</H2>
<%
String format = request.getParameter("format");
if ((format != null) && (format.equals("excel"))) {
  response.setContentType("application/vnd.ms-excel");
}
%>
<TABLE BORDER=1>
  <TR><TH></TH><TH>Apples<TH>Oranges
  <TR><TH>First Quarter<TD>2307<TD>4706
  <TR><TH>Second Quarter<TD>2982<TD>5104
  <TR><TH>Third Quarter<TD>3011<TD>5220
  <TR><TH>Fourth Quarter<TD>3055<TD>5287
</TABLE>

</CENTER>
</BODY>
</HTML>
```

## Notes:

___

___

___

___

___

___

## Apples and Oranges: Default Result

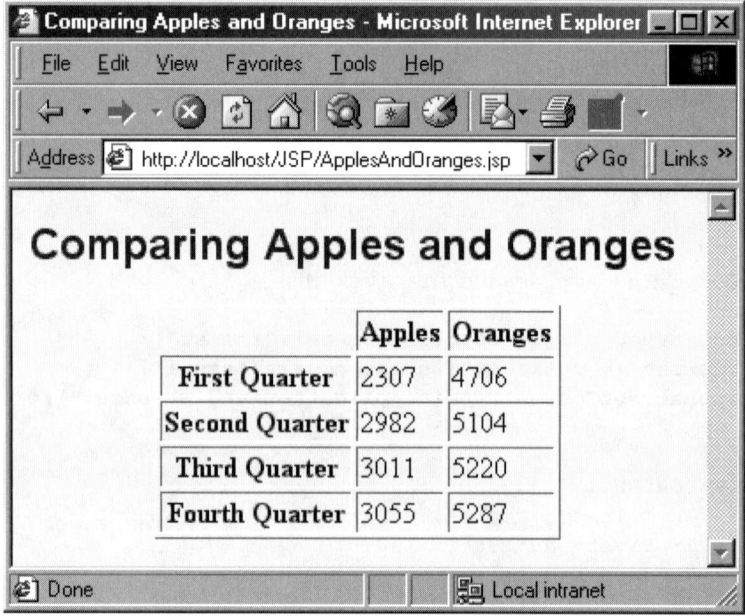

**Notes:**

## Apples and Oranges: Result with format=excel

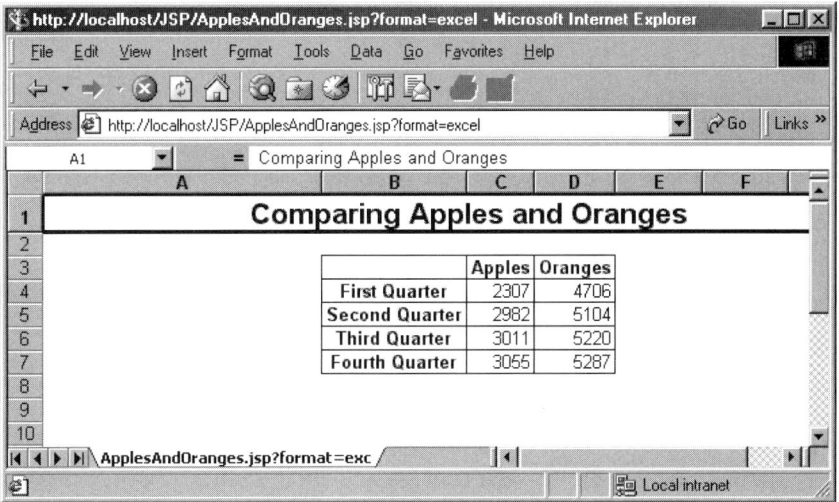

Notes:

## The isThreadSafe Attribute

- **Format**
  - <%@ page isThreadSafe="true" %> <%!-- Default --%>
  - <%@ page isThreadSafe="false" %>
- **Purpose**
  - To tell the system when your code is not threadsafe, so that the system can prevent concurrent access.
- **Notes**
  - Default is true—system assumes you have synchronized updates to fields and other shared data.
  - Supplying a value of false can degrade performance.
  - Systems are permitted to make multiple instances of the servlet class as long as each is called serially.
    Moral: static fields are not necessarily safe.

## Notes:

## Example of Non-Threadsafe Code (IDs Must Be Unique)

- **What's wrong with this code?**

```
<%! private int idNum = 0; %>
<%
String userID = "userID" + idNum;
out.println("Your ID is " + userID + ".");
idNum = idNum + 1;
%>
```

## Notes:

## Is isThreadSafe Needed Here?

- **No**
  ```
  <%! private int idNum = 0; %>
  <%
  synchronized(this) {
    String userID = "userID" + idNum;
    out.println("Your ID is " + userID + ".");
    idNum = idNum + 1;
  }
  %>
  ```
- **Totally safe, better performance in high-traffic environments**

## Notes:

## The session Attribute

- **Format**
  - <%@ page session="true" %> <%-- Default --%>
  - <%@ page session="false" %>
- **Purpose**
  - To designate that page not be part of a session.
- **Notes**
  - By default, it is part of a session.
  - Possible small performance gain in specifying false.

## Notes:

## The buffer Attribute

- **Format**
  - <%@ page buffer="*size*kb" %>
  - <%@ page buffer="none" %>
- **Purpose**
  - To give the size of the buffer used by the out variable.
- **Notes**
  - Buffering lets you set HTTP headers even after some page content has been generated (as long as buffer has not filled up or been explicitly flushed).
  - Servers are allowed to use a larger size than you ask for, but not a smaller size.
  - Default is system-specific, but must be at least 8kb.

## Notes:

## The autoflush Attribute

- **Format**
  - <%@ page autoflush="true" %> <%-- Default --%>
  - <%@ page autoflush="false" %>
- **Purpose**
  - To designate if buffer should be flushed when full (true) or if an exception should be raised (false).
- **Notes**
  - A value of false is illegal when also using buffer="none".

## Notes:

## The extends Attribute

- **Format**
  - <%@ page extends="package.class" %>
- **Purpose**
  - To specify parent class of servlet that will result from JSP page.
- **Notes**
  - Use with extreme caution.
  - Can prevent system from using high-performance custom superclasses.

## Notes:

## The errorPage Attribute

- **Format**
  - <%@ page errorPage="Relative URL" %>
- **Purpose**
  - Specifies a JSP page that should process any exceptions thrown but not caught in the current page.
- **Notes**
  - The exception thrown will be automatically available to the designated error page by means of the "exception" variable.

## Notes:

## The isErrorPage Attribute

- **Format**
  - <%@ page isErrorPage="true" %>
  - <%@ page isErrorPage="false" %> <%!-- Default --%>
- **Purpose**
  - Indicates whether or not the current page can act as the error page for another JSP page.
- **Notes**
  - Use this for emergency backup only; explicitly handle as many exceptions as possible.
  - Don't forget to always check query data for missing or malformed values.

## Notes:

## Error Pages: Example (ComputeSpeed.jsp)

```
...
<BODY>

<%@ page errorPage="SpeedErrors.jsp" %>

<TABLE BORDER=5 ALIGN="CENTER">
  <TR><TH CLASS="TITLE">
    Computing Speed
</TABLE>

<%!
// Note lack of try/catch for NumberFormatException
private double toDouble(String value) {
  return(Double.valueOf(value).doubleValue());
}
%>

<%
double furlongs =
  toDouble(request.getParameter("furlongs"));
double fortnights =
  toDouble(request.getParameter("fortnights"));
double speed = furlongs/fortnights;
%>

<UL>
  <LI>Distance: <%= furlongs %> furlongs.
  <LI>Time: <%= fortnights %> fortnights.
  <LI>Speed: <%= speed %> furlongs per fortnight.
</UL>
...
```

## Error Pages: Example (SpeedErrors.jsp)

```
...
<BODY>

<%@ page isErrorPage="true" %>

<TABLE BORDER=5 ALIGN="CENTER">
  <TR><TH CLASS="TITLE">
      Error Computing Speed</TABLE>
<P>
ComputeSpeed.jsp reported the following error:
<I><%= exception %></I>. This problem occurred in the
following place:
<PRE>
<% exception.printStackTrace(new PrintWriter(out)); %>
</PRE>
...
```

## Notes:

## LECTURE 9   THE JSP PAGE DIRECTIVE

# Error Pages: Example

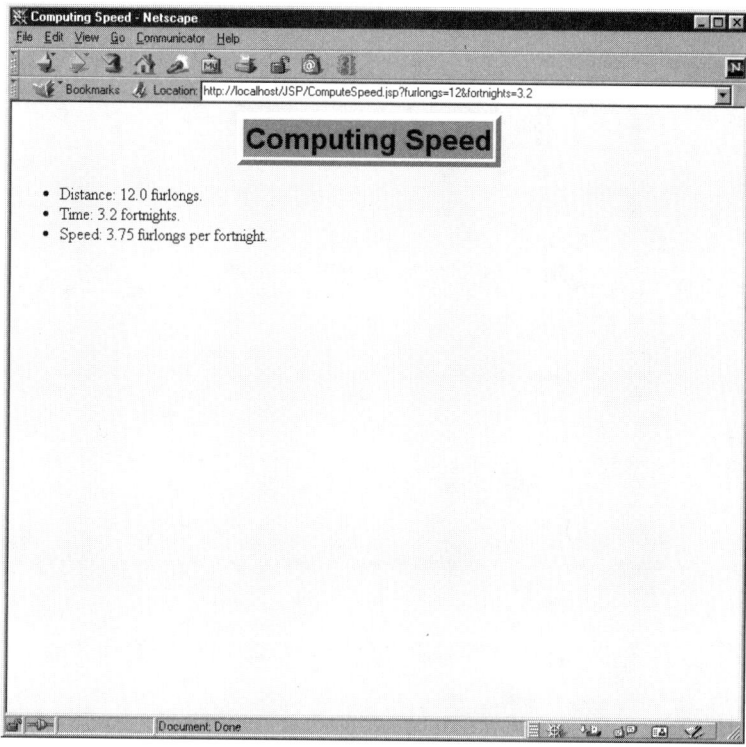

# Notes:

## Error Pages: Example

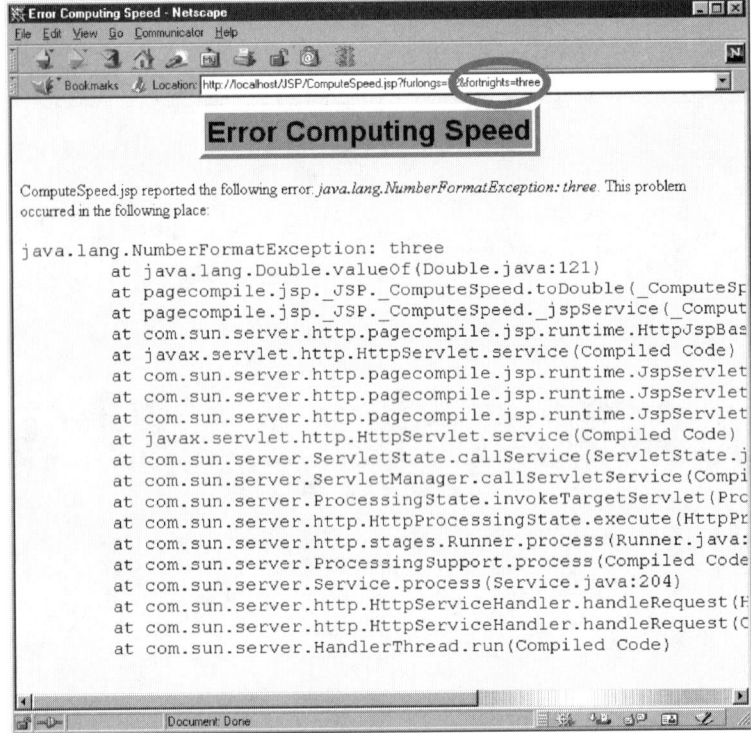

## Notes:

## Summary

- **The import attribute**
  - Changes the packages imported by the servlet that result from the JSP page.
- **The contentType attribute**
  - Specifies MIME type of result.
  - Cannot be used conditionally.
    - Use <% response.setContentType(...); %> instead.
- **The isThreadSafe attribute**
  - Turns off concurrent access.
  - Consider explicit synchronization instead.
- **The errorPage and isErrorPage attributes**
  - Specifies "emergency" error handling pages.

## Notes:

# Lecture 10

# Including Files and Applets in JSP Documents

## Agenda

- Including JSP files at the time the main page is translated into a servlet
- Including JSP, HTML or plain text files at the time the client requests the page
- Including applets that use the Java Plug-In

**Notes:**

# Including Files at Page Translation Time

- **Format**
  - <%@ include file="Relative URL" %>
- **Purpose**
  - To reuse JSP content in multiple pages, where JSP content affects main page.
- **Notes**
  - Servers are not required to detect changes to the included file, and in practice they don't.
  - Thus, you need to change the JSP files whenever the included file changes.
  - You can use OS-specific mechanisms such as the Unix "touch" command, or
    - **<%-- Navbar.jsp modified 3/1/00 --%>**
      <%@ include file="Navbar.jsp" %>

**Notes:**

## Reusable JSP Content: ContactSection.jsp

```jsp
<%@ page import="java.util.Date" %>
<%-- The following become fields in each servlet that
     results from a JSP page that includes this file. --%>
<%!
private int accessCount = 0;
private Date accessDate = new Date();
private String accessHost = "<I>No previous access</I>";
%>
<P>
<HR>
This page &copy; 2000
<A HREF="http://www.my-company.com/">my-company.com</A>.
This page has been accessed <%= ++accessCount %>
times since server reboot. It was last accessed from
<%= accessHost %> at <%= accessDate %>.
<% accessHost = request.getRemoteHost(); %>
<% accessDate = new Date(); %>
```

## Notes:

# LECTURE 10 INCLUDING FILES AND APPLETS IN JSP DOCUMENTS

## Using the JSP Content

```
...
<BODY>
<TABLE BORDER=5 ALIGN="CENTER">
  <TR><TH CLASS="TITLE">
      Some Random Page</TABLE>
<P>
Information about our products and services.
<P>
Blah, blah, blah.
<P>
Yadda, yadda, yadda.

<%@ include file="ContactSection.jsp" %>

</BODY>
</HTML>
```

## Notes:

## Using the JSP Content: Result

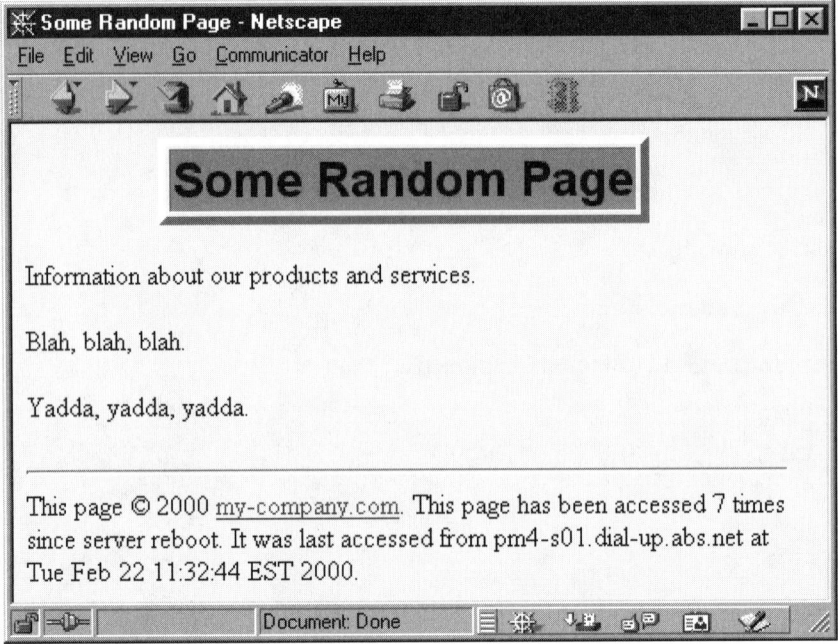

**Notes:**

## Including Files at Request Time

- **Format**
  - <jsp:include page="Relative URL" flush="true" />
- **Purpose**
  - To reuse JSP, HTML, or plain text content.
  - JSP content cannot affect main page:
    only *output* of included JSP page is used.
  - To permit updates to the included content without changing the main JSP page(s).
- **Notes**
  - The flush attribute can be omitted in JSP 1.1.
  - You are not permitted to specify false for the flush attribute.

**Notes:**

## Including Files: Example Code

```
...
<BODY>
<CENTER>
<TABLE BORDER=5>
  <TR><TH CLASS="TITLE">
      What's New at JspNews.com</TABLE>
</CENTER>
<P>
Here is a summary of our four most recent news stories:
<OL>
  <LI><jsp:include page="news/Item1.html" flush="true" />
  <LI><jsp:include page="news/Item2.html" flush="true" />
  <LI><jsp:include page="news/Item3.html" flush="true" />
  <LI><jsp:include page="news/Item4.html" flush="true" />
</OL>
</BODY></HTML>
```

## Notes:

# LECTURE 10 INCLUDING FILES AND APPLETS IN JSP DOCUMENTS

## Including Files: Example Result

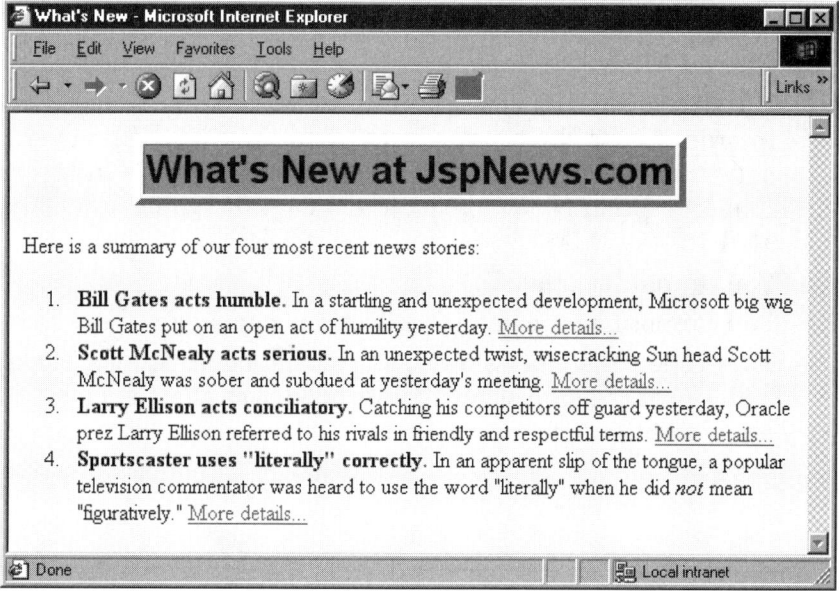

## Notes:

## Including Applets for the Java Plug-In

- **Netscape 4 and IE 5 do not support Java 2**
  — Netscape 6 supports JDK 1.3.
- **Problems using applets**
  — In order to use Swing, you must send the Swing files over the network. This process is time consuming and fails in Internet Explorer 3 and Netscape 3.x and 4.01-4.05 (which only support JDK 1.02).
  — You cannot use Java 2D.
  — You cannot use the Java 2 collections package.
  — Your code runs more slowly, since most compilers for the Java 2 platform are significantly improved over their 1.1 predecessors.

## Notes:

## Solution (?): Use the Java Plug-In

- **Only a viable option for intranets**
  — Requires *each* client to install large browser plug-in.
- **Cannot use simple APPLET tag**
- **Need long and ugly OBJECT tag for Internet Explorer**
- **Need long and ugly EMBED tag for Netscape**
- **The jsp:plugin action lets you write a simple tag that gets translated into the OBJECT and EMBED tags that are required**

## Notes:

## Using jsp:plugin

- **APPLET Tag**
  ```
  - <APPLET CODE="MyApplet.class"
           WIDTH=475 HEIGHT=350>
    </APPLET>
  ```
- **Equivalent jsp:include**
  ```
  <jsp:plugin type="applet"
              code="MyApplet.class"
              width="475" height="350">
  </jsp:plugin>
  ```
- **Reminder**
  — JSP element and attribute names are case sensitive.
  — All attribute values must be in single or double quotes.
  — This is like XML but unlike HTML.

## Notes:

## Attributes of the jsp:plugin Element

- **type**
  - For applets, this should be "applet."
    Use "bean" to embed JavaBeans elements in Web pages.
- **code**
  - Used identically to CODE attribute of APPLET, specifying the top-level applet class file.
- **width, height**
  - Used identically to WIDTH, HEIGHT in APPLET.
- **codebase**
  - Used identically to CODEBASE attribute of APPLET.
- **align**
  - Used identically to ALIGN in APPLET and IMG.
- **hspace, vspace**
  - Used identically to HSPACE, VSPACE in APPLET.
- **archive**
  - Used identically to ARCHIVE attribute of APPLET, specifying a JAR file from which classes and images should be loaded.
- **name**
  - Used identically to NAME attribute of APPLET, specifying a name to use for inter-applet communication or for identifying applet to scripting languages like JavaScript.
- **title**
  - Used identically to rarely used TITLE attribute.
- **jreversion**
  - Identifies version of the Java Runtime Environment (JRE) that is required. Default is 1.1.
- **iepluginurl**
  - Designates a URL from which plug-in for Internet Explorer can be downloaded. Users who don't already have the plug-in installed will be prompted to download it from this location. Default value will direct user to Sun site, but for intranet use you might want to direct user to a local copy.
- **nspluginurl**
  - Designates a URL from which plug-in for Netscape can be downloaded. Default value will direct user to Sun site, but for intranet use you might want local copy.

## The jsp:param and jsp:params Elements

- **PARAM Tags**
  — ```
    <APPLET CODE="MyApplet.class"
            WIDTH=475 HEIGHT=350>
      <PARAM NAME="PARAM1" VALUE="VALUE1">
      <PARAM NAME="PARAM2" VALUE="VALUE2">
    </APPLET>
    ```
- **Equivalent jsp:param**
  — ```
    <jsp:plugin type="applet"
                code="MyApplet.class"
                width="475" height="350">
      <jsp:params>
        <jsp:param name="PARAM1" value="VALUE1" />
        <jsp:param name="PARAM2" value="VALUE2" />
      </jsp:params>
    </jsp:plugin>
    ```

**Notes:**

## The jsp:fallback Element

- **APPLET Tag**
  - ```
    <APPLET CODE="MyApplet.class"
            WIDTH=475 HEIGHT=350>
      <B>Error: this example requires Java.</B>
    </APPLET>
    ```
- **Equivalent jsp:plugin with jsp:fallback**
  - ```
    <jsp:plugin type="applet"
                code="MyApplet.class"
                width="475" height="350">
      <jsp:fallback>
        <B>Error: this example requires Java.</B>
      </jsp:fallback>
    </jsp:plugin>
    ```

## Notes:

## Example Using Plugin

```
<DOCTYPE ...>
...
<jsp:plugin
    type="applet"
    code="coreservlets.ShadowedTextApplet.class"
    width="475" height="350">
  <jsp:params>
    <jsp:param name="MESSAGE"
               value="Your Message Here" />
  </jsp:params>
</jsp:plugin>
...
</BODY></HTML>
```

- **See book and Web site for applet code**

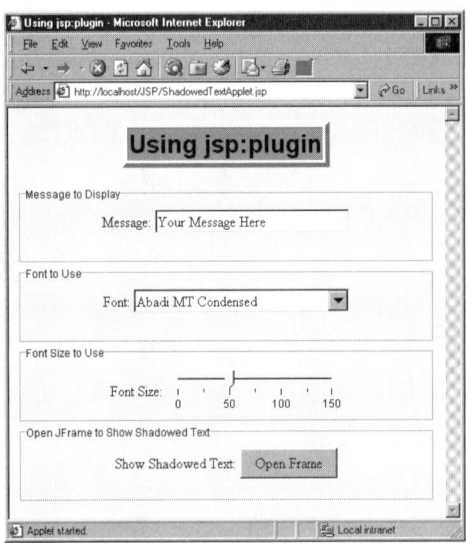 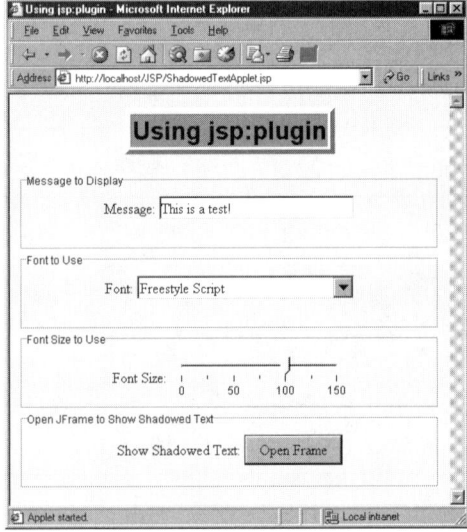

# LECTURE 10 INCLUDING FILES AND APPLETS IN JSP DOCUMENTS

## Example Using Plugin (continued)

## Notes:

## Summary

- **<%@ include file="Relative URL" %>**
  - File gets inserted into JSP page prior to page translation.
  - Thus, file can contain JSP content that affects entire page (e.g., import statements, declarations).
  - Changes to included file require you to manually update pages that use it.
- **<jsp:include page="Relative URL" flush="true" />**
  - Output of URL inserted into JSP page at request time.
  - Cannot contain JSP content that affects entire page.
  - Changes to included file do not necessitate changes to pages that use it.
- **<jsp:plugin ...> simplifies applets for plugin**

## Notes:

# Lecture 11

# Using JavaBeans with JSP

## Agenda

- Overview of beans in Java
- Basic use of beans in JSP
- Creating and accessing beans
- Setting bean properties explicitly
- Associating individual bean properties with request parameters
- Associating all bean properties with request parameters
- Conditional bean operations
- Sharing beans among multiple JSP pages and servlets

## Notes:

## Uses of JSP Constructs

Simple Application
↓
Complex Application

- Scripting elements calling servlet code directly
- Scripting elements calling servlet code indirectly (by means of utility classes)
- *Beans*
- Custom tags
- Servlet/JSP combo (with beans)

**Notes:**

## Background: What Are Beans?

- **Java classes that follow certain conventions**
  - Must have a zero-argument (empty) constructor.
    - You can satisfy this requirement either by explicitly defining such a constructor or by omitting all constructors.
  - Should have no public instance variables (fields).
    - I hope you already follow this practice and use accessor methods instead of allowing direct access to fields.
  - Persistent values should be accessed through methods called get*Xxx* and set*Xxx*.
    - If class has method getTitle that returns a String, class is said to have a String *property* named title.
    - Boolean properties use is*Xxx* instead of get*Xxx*.
  - For more on beans, see http://java.sun.com/beans/docs/.

## Notes:

## LECTURE 11  USING JAVABEANS WITH JSP

## Why You Should Use Accessors, Not Public Fields

- **To be a bean, you cannot have public fields**
- **So, you should replace**
  ```
  public double speed;
  ```
- **with**
  ```
  private double speed;
  public double getSpeed() {
    return(speed);
  }
  public void setSpeed(double newSpeed) {
    speed = newSpeed;
  }
  ```
- **You should do this in *all* your Java code anyhow. Why?**
  - **1) You can put constraints on values**
    ```
    public void setSpeed(double newSpeed) {
      if (newSpeed < 0) {
        sendErrorMessage(...);
        newSpeed = Math.abs(newSpeed);
      }
      speed = newSpeed;
    }
    ```
    — If users of your class accessed the fields directly, then they would each be responsible for checking constraints.
  - **2) You can change your internal representation without changing interface**
    ```
    // Now using metric units (kph, not mph)

    public void setSpeed(double newSpeed) {
      setSpeedInKPH = convert(newSpeed);
    }

    public void setSpeedInKPH(double newSpeed) {
      speedInKPH = newSpeed;
    }
    ```
  - **3) You can perform arbitrary side effects**
    ```
    public double setSpeed(double newSpeed) {
      speed = newSpeed;
      updateSpeedometerDisplay();
    }
    ```
    — If users of your class accessed the fields directly, then they would each be responsible for executing side effects. Too much work runs a huge risk of having display inconsistent from actual values.

## Basic Bean Use in JSP

- **Format**
  - <jsp:useBean id="*name*" class="*package.Class*" />
- **Purpose**
  - Allow instantiation of Java classes without explicit Java programming (XML-compatible syntax).
- **Notes**
  - Simple interpretation: JSP action.
    <jsp:useBean id="book1" class="coreservlets.Book" />
    can be thought of as equivalent to the scriptlet
    <% coreservlets.Book book1 = new coreservlets.Book(); %>
  - But useBean has two additional features.
    - Bean stored where other servlets/JSP pages can find it.
    - Existing bean of same name sometimes used.

**Notes:**

## Accessing Bean Properties

- **Format**
  - <jsp:getProperty name="*name*" property="*property*" />
- **Purpose**
  - Allow access to bean properties (i.e., calls to get*Xxx* methods) without explicit Java programming.
- **Notes**
  - <jsp:getProperty name="book1" property="title" />
    is equivalent to the following JSP expression
    <%= book1.getTitle() %>

## Notes:

## Setting Bean Properties: Simple Case

- **Format**
  - <jsp:setProperty name="*name*"
                    property="*property*"
                    value="*value*" />
- **Purpose**
  - Allow setting of bean properties (i.e., calls to set*Xxx* methods) without explicit Java programming.
- **Notes**
  - <jsp:setProperty name="book1"
              property="title"
              value="Core Servlets and JavaServer Pages" />
    is equivalent to the following scriptlet
    <% book1.setTitle("Core Servlets and JavaServer Pages"); %>

## Notes:

## Example: StringBean

```
package coreservlets;

public class StringBean {
  private String message = "No message specified";

  public String getMessage() {
    return(message);
  }

  public void setMessage(String message) {
    this.message = message;
  }
}
```

- **Installed in normal servlet directory**
  — E.g., C:\jakarta-tomcat\webapps\ROOT\WEB-INF\classes\coreservlets.

## Notes:

## JSP Page that Uses StringBean

```
<jsp:useBean id="stringBean"
             class="coreservlets.StringBean" />
<OL>
<LI>Initial value (getProperty):
    <I><jsp:getProperty name="stringBean"
                        property="message" /></I>
<LI>Initial value (JSP expression):
    <I><%= stringBean.getMessage() %></I>
<LI><jsp:setProperty name="stringBean"
                     property="message"
                     value="Best string bean: Fortex" />
    Value after setting property with setProperty:
    <I><jsp:getProperty name="stringBean"
                        property="message" /></I>
<LI><%stringBean.setMessage("My favorite: Kentucky Wonder");%>
    Value after setting property with scriptlet:
    <I><%= stringBean.getMessage() %></I>
</OL>
```

## Notes:

## LECTURE 11  USING JAVABEANS WITH JSP

## JSP Page that Uses StringBean

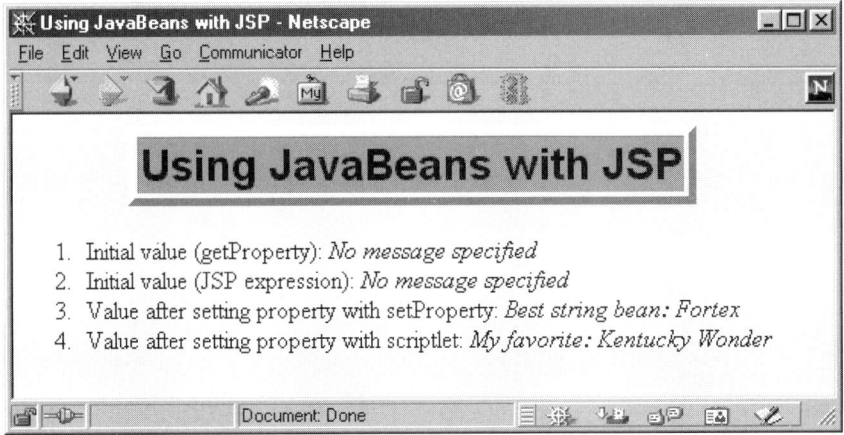

**Notes:**

## Setting Bean Properties Case 1: Explicit Conversion and Assignment

```
<!DOCTYPE ...>
...
<jsp:useBean id="entry"
             class="coreservlets.SaleEntry" />

<%-- getItemID expects a String --%>
<jsp:setProperty
    name="entry"
    property="itemID"
    value='<%= request.getParameter("itemID") %>' />

<%
int numItemsOrdered = 1;
try {
  numItemsOrdered =
    Integer.parseInt(request.getParameter("numItems"));
} catch(NumberFormatException nfe) {}
%>
<%-- getNumItems expects an int --%>
<jsp:setProperty
    name="entry"
    property="numItems"
    value="<%= numItemsOrdered %>" />

<%
double discountCode = 1.0;
try {
  String discountString =
    request.getParameter("discountCode");
  discountCode =
    Double.valueOf(discountString).doubleValue();
} catch(NumberFormatException nfe) {}
%>
<%-- getDiscountCode expects a double --%>
<jsp:setProperty
    name="entry"
    property="discountCode"
    value="<%= discountCode %>" />
```

## Setting Bean Properties Case 1:
## Explicit Conversion and Assignment (continued)

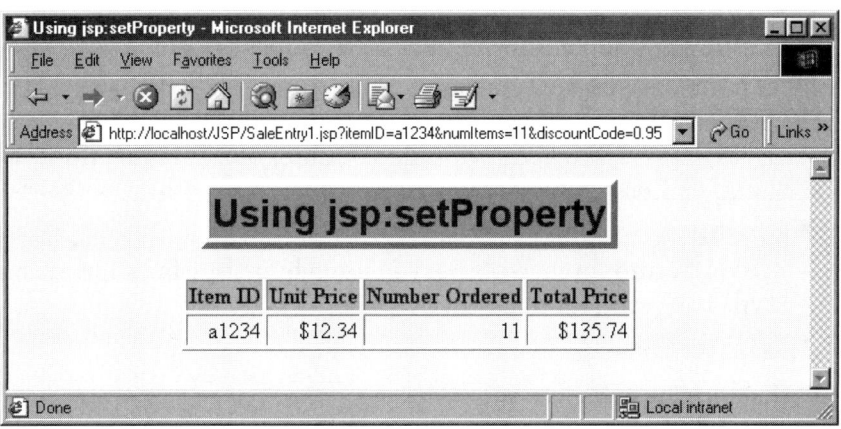

**Notes:**

## Case 2: Associating Individual Properties with Input Parameters

- **Use the param attribute of jsp:setProperty to indicate that**
  — Value should come from specified request parameter.
  — Simple automatic type conversion should be performed for properties that expect values of type boolean, Boolean, byte, Byte, char, Character, double, Double, int, Integer, float, Float, long, or Long.
- **Warning**
  — JSWDK and Java Web Server have bug that fails for automatic type conversions to double values.

```
<jsp:useBean id="entry"
             class="coreservlets.SaleEntry" />
<jsp:setProperty
    name="entry"
    property="itemID"
    param="itemID" />
<jsp:setProperty
    name="entry"
    property="numItems"
    param="numItems" />
<jsp:setProperty
    name="entry"
    property="discountCode"
    param="discountCode" />
```

## Notes:

## Case 3: Associating All Properties with Input Parameters

- **Use "*" for the value of the property attribute of jsp:setProperty to indicate that**
  — Value should come from request parameter whose name matches property name.
  — Simple automatic type conversion should be performed.

```
<jsp:useBean id="entry"
             class="coreservlets.SaleEntry" />
<jsp:setProperty name="entry" property="*" />
```

**Notes:**

## Sharing Beans

- **You can use scope Attribute to specify additional places where bean is stored**
  - Still also bound to local variable in _jspService (called by service).
- **Lets multiple servlets or JSP pages share data**
- **Also permits conditional bean creation**
  - Create new object only if you can't find existing one.

## Notes:

## Values of the Scope Attribute

- **page**
  — Default value. Bean object should be placed in the PageContext object for the duration of the current request. Lets other methods in same servlet access bean.
- **application**
  — Bean will be stored in ServletContext available through the predefined application variable or by call to getServletContext(). ServletContext is shared by all servlets in the same Web application (or all servlets on server if no explicit Web applications are defined). Values in the ServletContext can be accessed by getAttribute and setAttribute using the bean's id. This lets regular servlets interact with JSP beans. See section on integrating servlets and JSP.
- **session**
  — Bean will be stored in the HttpSession object associated with the current request, where it can be accessed from regular servlet code with getValue and putValue, as with normal session objects. Using scope="session" causes error at page translation time when page directive stipulates that current page is not using sessions.
- **request**
  — Bean object should be placed in the ServletRequest object for the duration of the current request, where it is available by means of getAttribute. This value is only a slight variation of the per-request scope provided by scope="page" (or by default when no scope is specified).

## Conditional Bean Operations

- **Bean conditionally created**
  - jsp:useBean results in new bean being instantiated only if no bean with same id and scope can be found.
  - If a bean with same id and scope is found, the preexisting bean is simply bound to variable referenced by id.
- **Bean properties conditionally set**
  - <jsp:useBean ... />
    replaced by
    <jsp:useBean ...>statements</jsp:useBean>
  - The statements (jsp:setProperty elements) are executed *only* if a new bean is created, not if an existing bean is found.

**Notes:**

## Conditional Bean Creation: AccessCountBean

```
package coreservlets;

public class AccessCountBean {
  private String firstPage;
  private int accessCount = 1;

  public String getFirstPage() {
    return(firstPage);
  }

  public void setFirstPage(String firstPage) {
    this.firstPage = firstPage;
  }

  public int getAccessCount() {
    return(accessCount++);
  }
}
```

**Notes:**

## Conditional Bean Creation: SharedCounts1.jsp

```
<jsp:useBean id="counter"
             class="coreservlets.AccessCountBean"
             scope="application">
  <jsp:setProperty name="counter"
                   property="firstPage"
                   value="SharedCounts1.jsp" />
</jsp:useBean>
Of SharedCounts1.jsp (this page),
<A HREF="SharedCounts2.jsp">SharedCounts2.jsp</A>, and
<A HREF="SharedCounts3.jsp">SharedCounts3.jsp</A>,
<jsp:getProperty name="counter" property="firstPage" />
was the first page accessed.
<P>
Collectively, the three pages have been accessed
<jsp:getProperty name="counter" property="accessCount" />
times.
```

## Notes:

## Accessing SharedCounts1, SharedCounts2, SharedCounts3

- **SharedCounts2.jsp was accessed first**
- **Pages have been accessed 12 previous times by an arbitrary number of clients**

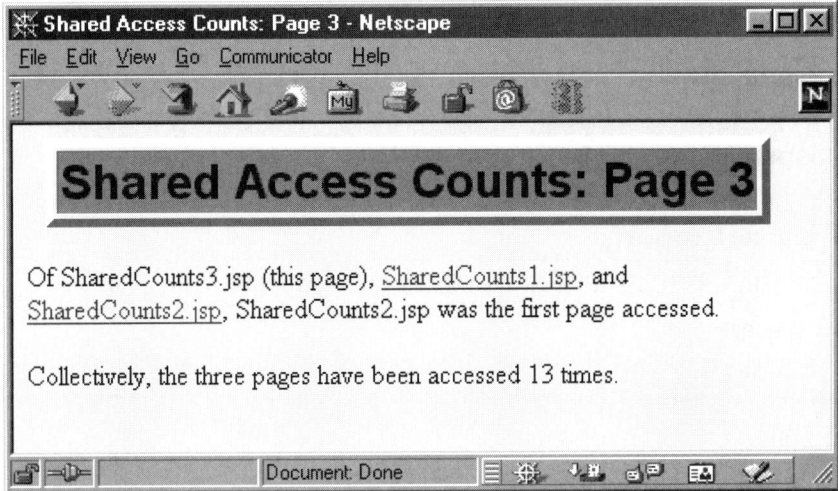

## Notes:

## Summary

- **Benefits of jsp:useBean**
  — Hides the Java syntax.
  — Makes it easier to associate request parameters with Java objects (bean properties).
  — Simplifies sharing objects among multiple requests or servlets/JSPs.
- **jsp:useBean**
  — Creates or accesses a bean.
- **jsp:getProperty**
  — Puts bean property (i.e., getXxx call) into servlet output.
- **jsp:setProperty**
  — Sets bean property (i.e., passes value to setXxx).

## Notes:

# Lecture 12

# Creating Custom JSP Tag Libraries

## Agenda

- **Components of a tag library**
- **Basic tags**
- **Tags that use attributes**
- **Tags that use body content**
- **Tags that optionally use body content**
- **Advanced tags**

**Notes:**

# LECTURE 12 CREATING CUSTOM JSP TAG LIBRARIES

## Uses of JSP Constructs

Simple
Application

Complex
Application

- Scripting elements calling servlet code directly
- Scripting elements calling servlet code indirectly (by means of utility classes)
- Beans
- *Custom tags*
- Servlet/JSP combo (with beans)

## Notes:

## Components that Make Up a Tag Library

- **The Tag Handler Class**
  - Java code that says how to actually translate tag into code.
  - Must implement javax.servlet.jsp.tagext.Tag interface.
  - Usually extends TagSupport or BodyTagSupport.
  - Goes in same directories as servlet class files and beans.
- **The Tag Library Descriptor File**
  - XML file describing tag name, attributes, and implementing tag handler class.
  - Goes with JSP file or at arbitrary URL.
- **The JSP File**
  - Imports a tag library (referencing URL of descriptor file).
  - Defines tag prefix.
  - Uses tags.

## Notes:

## Defining a Simple Tag Handler Class

- **Extend the TagSupport class**
- **Import needed packages**
  - import javax.servlet.jsp.*;
    import javax.servlet.jsp.tagext.*;
    import java.io.*;
- **Override doStartTag**
  - Obtain the JspWriter by means of pageContext.getOut().
  - Use the JspWriter to generate JSP content.
  - Return SKIP_BODY.
  - Translated into servlet code at page-translation time.
  - Code gets called at *request* time.

## Notes:

## Defining a Simple Tag Handler Class: Example

```java
package coreservlets.tags;
import javax.servlet.jsp.*;
import javax.servlet.jsp.tagext.*;
import java.io.*;
import java.math.*;
import coreservlets.*;

public class SimplePrimeTag extends TagSupport {
  protected int len = 50;

  public int doStartTag() {
    try {
      JspWriter out = pageContext.getOut();
      BigInteger prime = Primes.nextPrime(Primes.random(len));
      out.print(prime); // Primes class defined in Section 7.3
    } catch(IOException ioe) {
      System.out.println("Error generating prime: " + ioe);
    }
    return(SKIP_BODY);
  }}
```

## Notes:

## Defining a Simple Tag Library Descriptor

- **Start with XML header and DOCTYPE**
- **Top-level element is taglib**
- **Each tag defined by tag element containing:**
  - **name**, whose body defines the base tag name to which the prefix of the taglib directive will be attached. In this case, I use <name>simplePrime</name>
  - **tagclass**, which gives the fully qualified class name of the tag handler. In this case, I use <tagclass>coreservlets.tags.SimplePrimeTag</tagclass>
  - **info**, which gives a short description. Here, I use <info>Outputs a random 50-digit prime.</info>
  - **bodycontent**, which gives hints to development environments. Tomcat 3.1 doesn't support bodycontent. OK in JRun 3 and Tomcat 3.2.

**Notes:**

## TLD File for SimplePrimeTag

```
<?xml version="1.0" encoding="ISO-8859-1" ?>
<!DOCTYPE taglib PUBLIC
  "-//Sun Microsystems, Inc.//DTD JSP Tag Library 1.1//EN"
    "http://java.sun.com/j2ee/dtds/web-jsptaglibrary_1_1.dtd">
...
<taglib>
  <tag>
    <name>simplePrime</name>
    <tagclass>coreservlets.tags.SimplePrimeTag</tagclass>
    <info>Outputs a random 50-digit prime.</info>
  </tag>
</taglib>
```

- **Don't memorize XML header and DOCTYPE; modify version from coreservlets.com**

### Notes:

## Accessing Custom Tags from JSP Files

- **Import the tag library**
  - Specify location of TLD file
    <%@ taglib **uri="csajsp-taglib.tld"** prefix="csajsp" %>
  - Define a tag prefix (namespace)
    <%@ taglib uri="csajsp-taglib.tld" **prefix="csajsp"** %>
- **Use the tags**
  - <prefix:tagName />
    - Tag name comes from TLD file.
    - Prefix comes from taglib directive.
  - E.g., <csajsp:simplePrime />

## Notes:

## Using simplePrime Tag

```
...
<BODY>
<H1>Some 50-Digit Primes</H1>

<%@ taglib uri="csajsp-taglib.tld" prefix="csajsp" %>

<UL>
  <LI><csajsp:simplePrime />
  <LI><csajsp:simplePrime />
  <LI><csajsp:simplePrime />
  <LI><csajsp:simplePrime />
</UL>

</BODY>
</HTML>
```

## Notes:

# LECTURE 12 CREATING CUSTOM JSP TAG LIBRARIES

## Using simplePrime Tag: Result

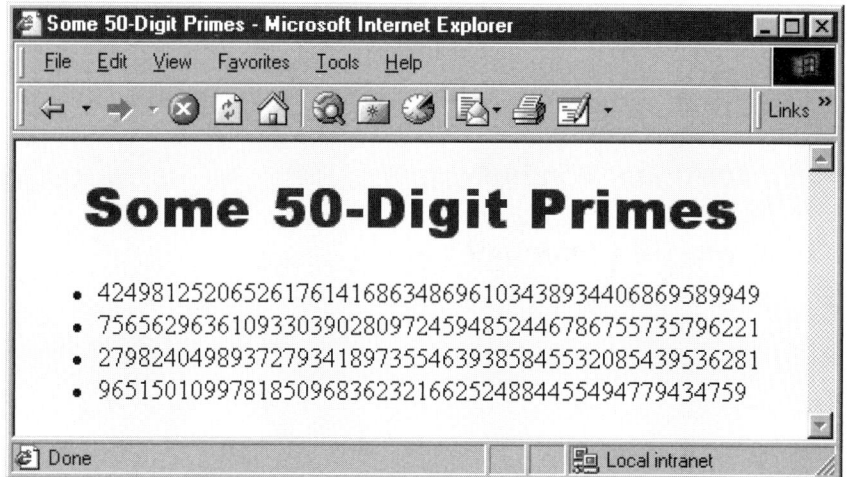

## Notes:

## Assigning Attributes to Tags

- **Allowing tags like**
  - <prefix:name
      **attribute1="value1"**.
      **attribute2="value2"**.
      ...
      **attributeN="valueN"**.
    />
- **Tags are still standalone**
  - No body between start and end tags.

**Notes:**

## Attributes: The Tag Handler Class

- **Use of an attribute called `attribute1` simply results in a call to a method called `setAttribute1`**
  — Attribute value is supplied to method as a String.
- **Example**
  — To support

    ```
    <prefix:tagName attribute1="Test" />
    ```

    add the following to tag handler class:

    ```
    public void setAttribute1(String value1) {
        doSomethingWith(value1);
    }
    ```

## Notes:

## Attributes: PrimeTag.java

```java
package coreservlets.tags;

import javax.servlet.jsp.*;
import javax.servlet.jsp.tagext.*;
import java.io.*;
import java.math.*;
import coreservlets.*;

public class PrimeTag extends SimplePrimeTag {
  public void setLength(String length) {
    try {
      len = Integer.parseInt(length); // Used by parent
    } catch(NumberFormatException nfe) {
      len = 50;
    }
  }
}
```

## Notes:

## Attributes: The Tag Library Descriptor File

- **The `tag` element must contain a nested `attribute` element**
- **The `attribute` element has three further-nested elements**
  - **name**, a required element that defines the case-sensitive attribute name. In this case, I use <name>length</name>
  - **required**, a required element that stipulates whether the attribute must always be supplied (true) or is optional (false). Here, to indicate that length is optional, I use <required>false</required>
  - **rtexprvalue**, an optional attribute that indicates whether the attribute value can be a JSP expression like <%= expression %> (true) or whether it must be a fixed string (false). The default value is false.

## Notes:

## TLD File for PrimeTag

```
...
<taglib>
  <tag>
    <name>prime</name>
    <tagclass>coreservlets.tags.PrimeTag</tagclass>
    <info>Outputs a random N-digit prime.</info>
    <attribute>
      <name>length</name>
      <required>false</required>
    </attribute>
  </tag>
</taglib>
```

## Notes:

## Using prime Tag

```html
...
<BODY>
<H1>Some N-Digit Primes</H1>

<%@ taglib uri="csajsp-taglib.tld" prefix="csajsp" %>

<UL>
  <LI>20-digit: <csajsp:prime length="20" />
  <LI>40-digit: <csajsp:prime length="40" />
  <LI>80-digit: <csajsp:prime length="80" />
  <LI>Default (50-digit): <csajsp:prime />
</UL>

</BODY>
</HTML>
```

## Notes:

## Using prime Tag: Result

**Notes:**

## Including the Tag Body

- **Simplest tags**
  - <prefix:tagName />
- **Tags with attributes**
  - <prefix:tagName att1="val1" ... />
- **Now**
  - <prefix:tagName>
    **JSP Content**
    </prefix:tagName>
  - <prefix:tagName att1="val1" ... />
    **JSP Content**
    </prefix:tagName>

## Notes:

## Using Tag Body: The Tag Handler Class

- **doStartTag**
  — Usually returns EVAL_BODY_INCLUDE instead of SKIP_BODY.
- **doEndTag**
  — Define this method if you want to take action after handling the body.
  — Return EVAL_PAGE.

**Notes:**

## Using Tag Body: HeadingTag.java

```java
package coreservlets.tags;
import javax.servlet.jsp.*;
import javax.servlet.jsp.tagext.*;
import java.io.*;

public class HeadingTag extends TagSupport {
  private String bgColor; // The one required attribute
  private String color = null;
  ...

  public void setBgColor(String bgColor) {
    this.bgColor = bgColor;
  }

  public void setColor(String color) {
    this.color = color;
  }
  ...

  public int doStartTag() {
    try {
      JspWriter out = pageContext.getOut();
      out.print("<TABLE BORDER=" + border +
                " BGCOLOR=\"" + bgColor + "\"" +
                " ALIGN=\"" + align + "\"");
      if (width != null) {
        out.print(" WIDTH=\"" + width + "\"");
      }
      ...
    } catch(IOException ioe) {
      System.out.println("Error in HeadingTag: " + ioe);
    }
    return(EVAL_BODY_INCLUDE); // Include tag body
  }

  public int doEndTag() {
    try {
      JspWriter out = pageContext.getOut();
      out.print("</SPAN></TABLE>");
    } catch(IOException ioe) {
      System.out.println("Error in HeadingTag: " + ioe);
    }
    return(EVAL_PAGE); // Continue with rest of JSP page
  }
```

## Using Tag Body: The Tag Library Descriptor File

- **Only difference is bodycontent element**
  — Should be JSP instead of empty.
- **Tomcat 3.1 does not support bodycontent**
  — Fixed in Tomcat 3.2. Also OK in JRun 3.
- **Purpose is primarily for development environments**
- **I will omit in my examples**

**Notes:**

## TLD File for HeadingTag

```
  ...
<taglib>
  <tag>
    <name>heading</name>
    <tagclass>coreservlets.tags.HeadingTag</tagclass>
    <info>Outputs a 1-cell table used as a heading.</info>
    <attribute>
      <name>bgColor</name>
      <required>true</required> <!-- bgColor is required -->
    </attribute>
    <attribute>
      <name>color</name>
      <required>false</required>
    </attribute>
    ...
  </tag>
</taglib>
```

## Notes:

## Using heading Tag

```
<%@ taglib uri="csajsp-taglib.tld" prefix="csajsp" %>
<csajsp:heading bgColor="#C0C0C0">
Default Heading
</csajsp:heading>
<P>
<csajsp:heading bgColor="BLACK" color="WHITE">
White on Black Heading
</csajsp:heading>
<P>
<csajsp:heading bgColor="#EF8429" fontSize="60" border="5">
Large Bordered Heading
</csajsp:heading>
<P>
<csajsp:heading bgColor="CYAN" width="100%">
Heading with Full-Width Background
</csajsp:heading>
...
```

## Notes:

# Using heading Tag: Result

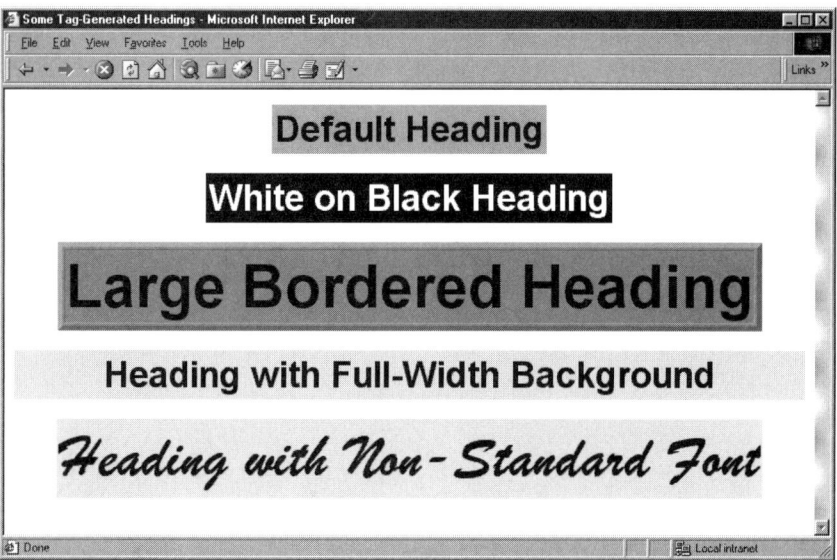

**Notes:**

## Optional Tag Bodies

- **First examples had no tag bodies**
  - doStartTag returned SKIP_BODY.
- **Most recent examples always included tag bodies**
  - doStartTag returned EVAL_BODY_INCLUDE.
- **Now: decide whether or not to include tag body at request time**
  - Have doStartTag return either SKIP_BODY or EVAL_BODY_INCLUDE depending on values of request time information.

**Notes:**

## Optional Tag Bodies: DebugTag.java

```java
package coreservlets.tags;
import javax.servlet.jsp.*;
import javax.servlet.jsp.tagext.*;
import java.io.*;
import javax.servlet.*;

public class DebugTag extends TagSupport {
  public int doStartTag() {
    ServletRequest request = pageContext.getRequest();
    String debugFlag = request.getParameter("debug");
    if ((debugFlag != null) &&
        (!debugFlag.equalsIgnoreCase("false"))) {
      return(EVAL_BODY_INCLUDE);
    } else {
      return(SKIP_BODY);
    }
}}
```

## Notes:

## TLD File for DebugTag

```
...
<taglib>
  <tag>
    <name>debug</name>
    <tagclass>coreservlets.tags.DebugTag</tagclass>
    <info>
    Includes body only if debug param is set.
    </info>
  </tag>
</taglib>
```

## Notes:

## LECTURE 12 CREATING CUSTOM JSP TAG LIBRARIES

# Using debug Tag

```
<%@ taglib uri="csajsp-taglib.tld" prefix="csajsp" %>
Top of regular page. Blah, blah, blah.
Yadda, yadda, yadda.
<P>
<csajsp:debug>
<B>Debug:</B>
<UL>
  <LI>Current time: <%= new java.util.Date() %>
  <LI>Requesting hostname: <%= request.getRemoteHost() %>
  <LI>Session ID: <%= session.getId() %>
</UL>
</csajsp:debug>
<P>
Bottom of regular page. Blah, blah, blah.
Yadda, yadda, yadda.
```

# Notes:

## Using debug Tag: Results

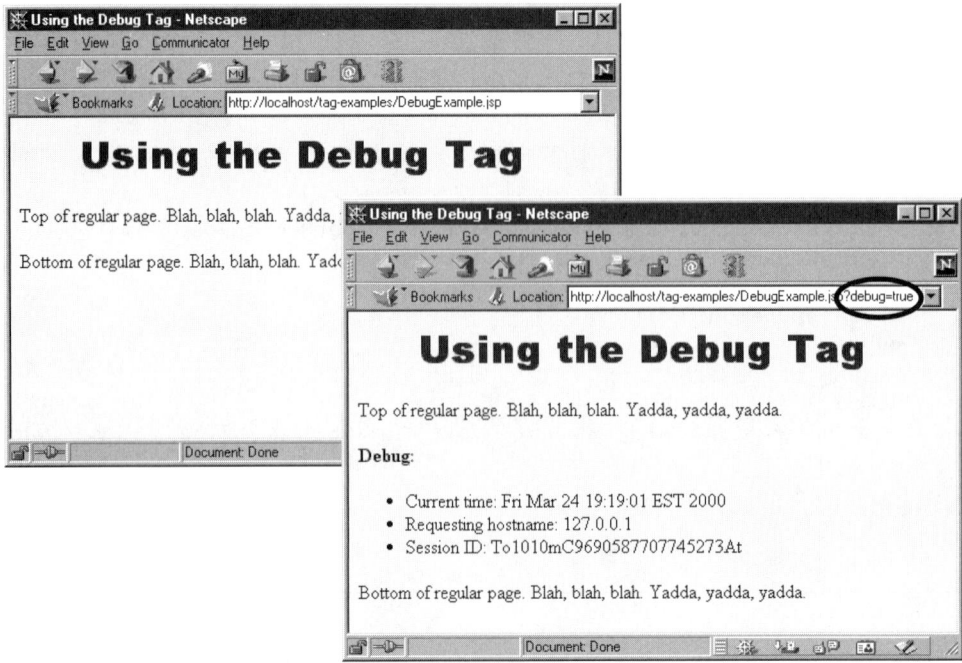

## Notes:

## Manipulating the Tag Body

- **No tag body**
  — <prefix:tagName />
  — <prefix:tagName att1="val1" ... />
- **Previous uses of tag body**
  — <prefix:tagName>JSP Content</prefix:tagName>
  — <prefix:tagName att1="val1" ... />
    JSP Content
    </prefix:tagName>
  — **Content inserted verbatim.**
- **Now**
  — Same JSP syntax for using a tag body.
  — **Java code can read/modify/replace tag body.**

## Notes:

## Manipulating Tag Body: The Tag Handler Class

- **Extend BodyTagSupport**
  — TagSupport does not have enough infrastructure to support reading/manipulating the tag body.
- **New method to override: doAfterBody**
  — Return SKIP_BODY when done.
- **getBodyContent returns object of typeBodyContent that has three key methods**
  — **getEnclosingWriter**—returns the JspWriter being used by doStartTag and doEndTag.
  — **getReader**—returns a Reader that can read tag's body.
  — **getString**—returns a String containing entire tag body.

**Notes:**

## LECTURE 12 CREATING CUSTOM JSP TAG LIBRARIES

## Manipulating Tag Body: FilterTag.java

```java
public class FilterTag extends BodyTagSupport {
  public int doAfterBody() {
    BodyContent body = getBodyContent();
    String filteredBody =
      // The filter method is defined in Section 3.6
      ServletUtilities.filter(body.getString());
    try {
      JspWriter out = body.getEnclosingWriter();
      out.print(filteredBody);
    } catch(IOException ioe) {
      System.out.println("Error in FilterTag: " + ioe);
    }
    // SKIP_BODY means I'm done. If I wanted to evaluate
    // and handle body again, I'd return EVAL_BODY_TAG.
    return(SKIP_BODY);
  }
}
```

## Notes:

## Manipulating Tag Body: The Tag Library Descriptor File

- **No new capabilities needed**

```
<tag>
  <name>filter</name>
  <tagclass>coreservlets.tags.FilterTag</tagclass>
  <info>
  Replaces HTML-specific
  characters in body.
  </info>
</tag>
```

**Notes:**

## Using filter Tag

```
...
<%@ taglib uri="csajsp-taglib.tld" prefix="csajsp" %>
<TABLE BORDER=1 ALIGN="CENTER">
<TR CLASS="COLORED"><TH>Example<TH>Result
<TR>
<TD><PRE><csajsp:filter>
<EM>Some emphasized text.</EM><BR>
<STRONG>Some strongly emphasized text.</STRONG><BR>
<CODE>Some code.</CODE><BR>
...
</csajsp:filter></PRE>

<TD>
<EM>Some emphasized text.</EM><BR>
<STRONG>Some strongly emphasized text.</STRONG><BR>
<CODE>Some code.</CODE><BR>
...
</TABLE>
```

## Notes:

## Using filter Tag: Results

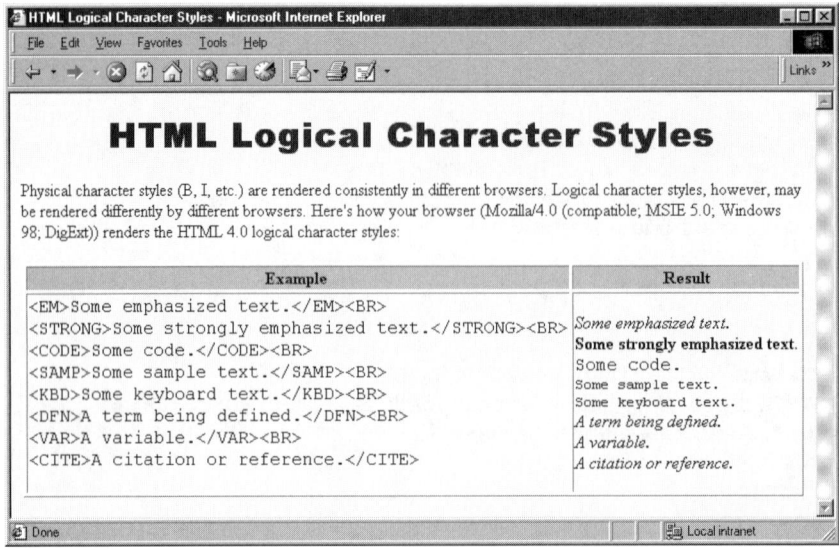

## Notes:

## Advanced Custom Tags

- **Manipulating the body multiple times**
  - Return EVAL_BODY_TAG from doAfterBody until last repetition.
  - Use the TLD file to specify that JSP expressions are permitted as attribute values.
- **Nested tags**
  - The handler for the inner tag uses findAncestorWithClass to get a reference to the enclosing tag handler.
- **Details and examples of both are given in the book**

## Notes:

## Summary

- **For each custom tag, you need**
  - A tag handler class (usually extending TagSupport or BodyTagSupport).
  - An entry in a Tag Library Descriptor file.
  - A JSP file that imports it, specifies prefix, and uses it.
- **Simple tags**
  - Generate output in doStartTag, return SKIP_BODY.
- **Attributes**
  - Define set*AttributeName* method. Update TLD file.
- **Body content**
  - doStartTag returns EVAL_BODY_INCLUDE.
  - Add doEndTag method.

## Notes:

# Lecture 13

# Integrating Servlets and JavaServer Pages

## Agenda

- **Reasons to combine servlets and JSP**
- **Approach to integration**
- **Dispatching requests**
- **Forwarding requests: an on-line travel agent**
- **Including requests: showing raw servlet and JSP output**

## Notes:

## Uses of JSP Constructs

Simple Application → Complex Application

- Scripting elements calling servlet code directly
- Scripting elements calling servlet code indirectly (by means of utility classes)
- Beans
- Custom tags
- *Servlet/JSP combo (with beans)*

Notes:

## Why Combine Servlets and JSP?

- **Typical picture: use JSP to make it easier to develop and maintain the HTML content**
  - For simple dynamic code, call servlet code from scripting elements.
  - For slightly more complex applications, use custom classes called from scripting elements.
  - For moderately complex applications, use beans and custom tags.
- **But, that's not enough**
  - For complex processing, starting with JSP is awkward.
  - Despite the ease of separating the real code into separate classes, beans, and custom tags, the assumption behind JSP is that a single page gives a single basic look.

**Notes:**

## Approach

- Original request is answered by a servlet
- Servlet processes request data, does database lookup, accesses business logic, etc.
- Results are placed in beans
- Request is forwarded to a JSP page to format result
- Different JSP pages can be used to handle different types of presentation
- Sometimes called the "Model 2" or "Model View Controller" approach to JSP
- See http://jakarta.apache.org/struts/ for code that supports this approach

## Notes:

## Dispatching Requests

- **First, call the getRequestDispatcher method of Servlet Context**
  — Supply URL relative to server or Web application root.
  — Example:
    - String url = "/presentations/presentation1.jsp";
      RequestDispatcher dispatcher =
      getServletContext().getRequestDispatcher(url);
- **Second**
  — Call **forward** to completely transfer control to destination page (no communication with client in between, as with response.sendRedirect).
  — Call **include** to insert output of destination page and then continue on.

## Notes:

_____

_____

_____

_____

_____

_____

## Forwarding Requests: Example Code

```
public void doGet(HttpServletRequest request,
                  HttpServletResponse response)
    throws ServletException, IOException {
  String operation = request.getParameter("operation");
  if (operation == null) {
    operation = "unknown";
  }
  if (operation.equals("operation1")) {
    gotoPage("/operations/presentation1.jsp",
             request, response);
  } else if (operation.equals("operation2")) {
    gotoPage("/operations/presentation2.jsp",
             request, response);
  } else {
    gotoPage("/operations/unknownRequestHandler.jsp",
             request, response);
  }
}

private void gotoPage(String address,
                      HttpServletRequest request,
                      HttpServletResponse response)
    throws ServletException, IOException {
  RequestDispatcher dispatcher =
    getServletContext().getRequestDispatcher(address);
  dispatcher.forward(request, response);
}
```

## Notes:

## Reminder: JSP useBean Scope Alternatives

- **request**
  - <jsp:useBean id="..." class="..." **scope="request"** />
- **session**
  - <jsp:useBean id="..." class="..." **scope="session"** />
- **application**
  - <jsp:useBean id="..." class="..." **scope="application"** />
- **page**
  - <jsp:useBean id="..." class="..." **scope="page"** />
    or just
    <jsp:useBean id="..." class="..." />
  - This scope is not used in Model 2 architecture.

## Notes:

## Storing Data for Later Use: The Servlet Request

- **Purpose**
  — Storing data that servlet looked up and that JSP page will use only in this request.
- **Servlet syntax to store data**
  ```
  SomeClass value = new SomeClass(…);
  request.setAttribute("key", value);
  ```
- **JSP syntax to retrieve data**
  ```
  <jsp:useBean
     id="key"
     class="SomeClass"
     scope="request" />
  ```

## Notes:

## Storing Data for Later Use: The Servlet Request (Variation)

- **Purpose**
  - Storing data that servlet looked up and that JSP page will use only in this request. *Servlets 2.2 only.*
- **Servlet syntax to store data**
  - Add new request parameters to servlet request.
    ```
    String address ="/path/resource.jsp?newParam=value";
    RequestDispatcher dispatcher =
      getServletContext().getRequestDispatcher(address);
    dispatcher.forward(request, response);
    ```
- **JSP syntax to retrieve data**
  - No useBean syntax. However, recall that request parameters can be accessed without explicit Java code by means of jsp:setProperty.

## Notes:

## Storing Data for Later Use: The Session Object

- **Purpose**
  — Storing data that servlet looked up and that JSP page will use in this request and in later requests from same client.
- **Servlet syntax to store data**
  ```
  SomeClass value = new SomeClass(...);
  HttpSession session =
    request.getSession(true);
  session.putValue("key", value);
  ```
- **JSP syntax to retrieve data**
  ```
  <jsp:useBean
     id="key"
     class="SomeClass"
     scope="session" />
  ```

## Notes:

## Storing Data for Later Use: The Servlet Context

- **Purpose**
  - Storing data that servlet looked up and that JSP page will use in this request and in later requests from *any* client.
- **Servlet syntax to store data**
  ```
  SomeClass value = new SomeClass(...);
  getServletContext().setAttribute("key", value);
  ```
- **JSP syntax to retrieve data**
  ```
  <jsp:useBean
    id="key"
    class="SomeClass"
    scope="application" />
  ```

## Notes:

# LECTURE 13  INTEGRATING SERVLETS AND JAVASERVER PAGES

## Example: An On-Line Travel Agent

- **All requests include**
  — Email address, password, trip origin, trip destination, start date, and end date.
- **Original request answered by servlet**
  — Looks up real name, address, credit card information, frequent flyer data, etc., using email address and password as key. *Data stored in session object.*
- **Depending on what button user pressed, request forwarded to:**
  — Page showing available flights, times, and costs.
  — Page showing available hotels, features, and costs.
  — Rental car info, edit customer data, error handler.

## An On-Line Travel Agent: Servlet Code

```
public void doPost(HttpServletRequest request,
                   HttpServletResponse response)
  ...// Store customer data in TravelCustomer bean
  HttpSession session = request.getSession(true);
  session.putValue("customer", customer);
  if (request.getParameter("flights") != null) {
    gotoPage("/travel/BookFlights.jsp",
             request, response);
  } else if ...
}
private void gotoPage(String address,
                      HttpServletRequest request,
                      HttpServletResponse response)
    throws ServletException, IOException {
  RequestDispatcher dispatcher =
    getServletContext().getRequestDispatcher(address);
  dispatcher.forward(request, response);
}
```

## Notes:

## An On-Line Travel Agent: JSP Code (Flight Page)

```
<BODY>
<H1>Best Available Flights</H1>
<CENTER>
<jsp:useBean id="customer"
             class="coreservlets.TravelCustomer"
             scope="session" />
Finding flights for
<jsp:getProperty name="customer"
                 property="fullName" />
<P>
<jsp:getProperty name="customer" property="flights" />
...
```

## Notes:

## Forwarding Requests from JSP Pages—jsp:forward

- **You usually forward from a servlet to a JSP page, but you can also forward from a JSP page**

```jsp
<% String destination;
   if (Math.random() > 0.5) {
     destination = "/examples/page1.jsp";
   } else {
     destination = "/examples/page2.jsp";
   }
%>
<jsp:forward page="<%= destination %>" />
```

## Notes:

## Including Pages Instead of Forwarding to Them

- **With the forward method of RequestDispatcher:**
  — Control is permanently transferred to new page.
  — Original page cannot generate any output.
- **With the include method of RequestDispatcher:**
  — Control is temporarily transferred to new page.
  — Original page can generate output before and after the included page.
  — Original servlet does not see the output of the included page ("servlet chaining" is not a standard capability).

## Notes:

## A Servlet that Shows Raw Servlet and JSP Output

```
             out.println(...
                        "<TEXTAREA ROWS=30 COLS=70>");
   if ((url == null) || (url.length() == 0)) {
     out.println("No URL specified.");
   } else {
     // Attaching data works only in version 2.2.
     String data = request.getParameter("data");
     if ((data != null) && (data.length() > 0)) {
       url = url + "?" + data;
     }
     RequestDispatcher dispatcher =
       getServletContext().getRequestDispatcher(url);
     dispatcher.include(request, response);
   }
   out.println("</TEXTAREA>\n" +
               ...);
```

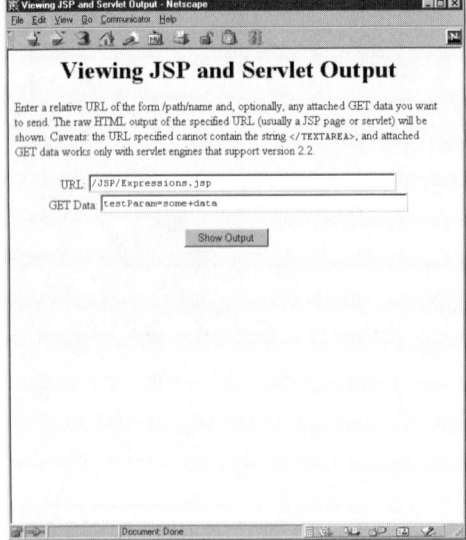 

## Summary

- **Use Model 2 approach when:**
  — One submission will result in more than one basic look.
  — Several pages have substantial common processing.
- **Architecture**
  — A servlet answers the original request.
  — Servlet does the real processing and stores results in beans.
    - Beans stored in HttpServletRequest, HttpSession, or ServletContext.
  — Servlet forwards to JSP page via forward method of RequestDispatcher.
  — JSP page reads data from beans by means of jsp:useBean with appropriate scope (request, session, or application).

## Notes:

# Lecture 14

# Servlet and JSP Summary

## Getting Started

- **Servlets are efficient, portable, powerful, and widely accepted in industry**
- **Regardless of deployment server, run a free server on your desktop for development**
- **Getting started:**
  — Set your CLASSPATH.
    - Servlet and JSP JAR files.
    - Top of your package hierarchy.
  — Put class files in proper location.
  — Use proper URL, usually http://*host*/servlet/ServletName.
- **Download existing servlet first time**
  — Start with HelloWWW from www.coreservlets.com.
- **Main servlet code goes in doGet or doPost:**
  — The HttpServletRequest contains the incoming information.
  — The HttpServletResponse lets you set outgoing information.
    - Call setContentType to specify MIME type.
    - Call getWriter to obtain a Writer pointing to client.
- **One-time setup code goes in init**
  — Servlet gets initialized and loaded once.
  — Servlet gets invoked multiple times.

**Notes:**

## LECTURE 14 SERVLET AND JSP SUMMARY

## Handling Form Data (Query Data)

- **Query data comes from HTML forms as URL-encoded name/value pairs**
- **Servlets read data by calling request.getParameter("name")**
  - Results in value as entered into form, not as sent over network. I.e., *not* URL-encoded.
- **Always check for missing or malformed data**
  - Special case: query data that contains special HTML characters.
    - Need to be filtered if query data will be placed into resultant HTML page.

## Notes:

## Using HTTP Request Headers

- **Many servlet tasks can *only* be accomplished by making use of HTTP headers coming from the browser**
- **Use request.getHeader for arbitrary header**
- **Cookies, authorization info, content length, and content type have shortcut methods**
- **Most important headers you read directly**
  — Accept.
  — Accept-Encoding.
  — Connection.
  — Referer.
  — User-Agent.

## Notes:

## Generating the HTTP Response

- **Many servlet tasks can *only* be accomplished through use of HTTP status codes and headers sent to the browser**
- **Two parts of the response**
  — Status line.
    - In general, set via response.setStatus.
    - In special cases, set via response.sendRedirect and response.sendError.
  — Response headers.
    - In general, set via response.setHeader.
    - In special cases, set via response.setContentType, response.setContentLength, response.addCookie, and response.sendRedirect.
- **Most important status codes**
  — 200 (default).
  — 302 (forwarding; set via sendRedirect).
  — 401 (password needed).
  — 404 (not found; set via sendError).
- **Most important headers you set directly**
  — Cache-Control and Pragma.
  — Content-Encoding.
  — Content-Length.
  — Expires.
  — Refresh.
  — WWW-Authenticate.

## Handling Cookies

- Cookies involve name/value pairs sent from server to browser and returned when the same page, site, or domain is visited later
- **Let you**
  - Track sessions (use higher-level API).
  - Permit users to avoid logging in at low-security sites.
  - Customize sites for different users.
  - Focus content or advertising.
- **Setting cookies**
  - Call Cookie constructor, set age, call response.addCookie.
- **Reading cookies**
  - Call request.getCookies, look through array for matching name, use associated value.

## Notes:

## Session Tracking

- **Although it usually uses cookies behind the scenes, the session tracking API is higher-level and easier to use than the cookie API**
- **Session information lives on server**
  — Cookie or extra URL info associates it with a user.
- **Obtaining session**
  — request.getSession(true).
- **Associating values with keys**
  — session.putValue (or session.setAttribute).
- **Finding values associated with keys**
  — session.getValue (or session.getAttribute).
    - Always check if this value is null before trying to use it.

## Notes:

## JSP Introduction

- **JSP makes it easier to create and maintain HTML, while still providing full access to servlet code**
- **JSP pages get translated into servlets**
  - It is the servlets that run at request time.
  - Client does not see *anything* JSP-related.
- **You still need to understand servlets**
  - Understanding how JSP really works.
  - Servlet code called from JSP.
  - Mixing servlets and JSP.
- **Other technologies use similar approach, but aren't as portable and don't let you use Java for the "real code"**

**Notes:**

## Uses of JSP Constructs

Simple Application
↓
Complex Application

- Scripting elements calling servlet code directly
- Scripting elements calling servlet code indirectly (by means of utility classes)
- Beans
- Custom tags
- Servlet/JSP combo (with beans)

**Notes:**

## Calling Java Code Directly: JSP Scripting Elements

- **JSP Expressions**
  — Format: <%= expression %>
  — Evaluated and inserted into the servlet's output.
- **JSP Scriptlets**
  — Format: <% code %>
  — Inserted verbatim into the servlet's _jspService method.
- **JSP Declarations**
  — Format: <%! code %>
  — Inserted verbatim into the body of the servlet class.
- **Predefined variables**
  — request, response, out, session, application.
- **Limit the Java code that is directly in page**
  — Use helper classes, beans, custom tags, servlet/JSP combo.

## Notes:

## The JSP page Directive: Structuring Generated Servlets

- **The import attribute**
  — Changes the packages imported by the servlet that results from the JSP page.
- **The contentType attribute**
  — Specifies MIME type of result.
  — Cannot be used conditionally.
    - Use <% response.setContentType(...); %> instead.
- **The isThreadSafe attribute**
  — Turns off concurrent access.
  — Consider explicit synchronization instead.
- **The errorPage and isErrorPage attributes**
  — Specifies "emergency" error handling pages.

**Notes:**

## Including Files and Applets in JSP Documents

- **<%@ include file="Relative URL" %>**
  — File gets inserted into JSP page prior to page translation.
  — Thus, file can contain JSP content that affects entire page (e.g., import statements, declarations).
  — Changes to included file require you to manually update pages that use it.
- **<jsp:include page="Relative URL"**
  **flush="true" />**
  — Output of URL inserted into JSP page at request time.
  — Cannot contain JSP content that affects entire page.
  — Changes to included file do not necessitate changes to pages that use it.
- **<jsp:plugin ...> simplifies applets for plugin**

### Notes:

## Using JavaBeans with JSP

- **Benefits of jsp:useBean**
  — Hides the Java syntax.
  — Makes it easier to associate request parameters with Java objects (bean properties).
  — Simplifies sharing objects among multiple requests or servlets/JSPs.
- **jsp:useBean**
  — Creates or accesses a bean.
- **jsp:getProperty**
  — Puts bean property (i.e., getXxx call) into servlet output.
- **jsp:setProperty**
  — Sets bean property (i.e., passes value to setXxx).

## Notes:

## Creating Custom JSP Tag Libraries

- **For each custom tag, you need**
  - A tag handler class (usually extending TagSupport or BodyTagSupport).
  - An entry in a Tag Library Descriptor file.
  - A JSP file that imports it, specifies prefix, and uses it.
- **Simple tags**
  - Generate output in doStartTag, return SKIP_BODY.
- **Attributes**
  - Define set*AttributeName* method. Update TLD file.
- **Body content**
  - doStartTag returns EVAL_BODY_INCLUDE.
  - Add doEndTag method.

## Notes:

## Integrating Servlets and JSP

- **Use Model 2 approach when**
  - One submission will result in more than one basic look.
  - Several pages have substantial common processing.
- **Architecture**
  - A servlet answers the original request.
  - Servlet does the real processing and stores results in beans.
    - Beans stored in HttpServletRequest, HttpSession, or ServletContext.
  - Servlet forwards to JSP page via forward method of RequestDispatcher.
  - JSP page reads data from beans by means of jsp:useBean with appropriate scope (request, session, or application).

## Notes:

## More Information

- **Source code for all examples**
  - http://www.coreservlets.com.
- ***Core Servlets and JavaServer Pages***
  - Sun Microsystems Press and Prentice Hall.
  - Order on-line or visit any bookstore with a large tech-books section.
- **Servlet home page**
  - http://java.sun.com/products/servlet/
- **JavaServer Pages home page**
  - http://java.sun.com/products/jsp/